Among the gre
management c
is the most de
experience, wis
spiritually proven path to assist leaders in every profession
transition effectively.

—JACK W. HAYFORD, CHANCELLOR
THE KING'S UNIVERSITY, LOS ANGELES

Dr. Naomi Dowdy has taken the axiom "No success without a successor" to a new level of understanding, using biblical insight, and applied it to her real-life experience. This makes her, in my eyes, a great mentor, and model of this restored apostolic truth. This is must-read for all—especially leaders.

—DR. JOHN P. KELLY
CEO, LEAD, ICWBF
PRESIDING APOSTLE, ICA

Many great leadership books on the market today contain helpful advice. But Naomi Dowdy offers more than advice here—she offers her life experiences as the leader of a church that is making a global impact. This book contains her life message, and I am thrilled that she has recorded it for all of us. It is a treasure chest of godly wisdom. All leaders will benefit from reading this important book.

—J. LEE GRADY, CHARISMA MAGAZINE
DIRECTOR, THE MORDECAI PROJECT

The questions Dr. Naomi Dowdy poses in this book will cut to the core of who you are as a leader, forcing the leader to take a good hard look at succession and examining the motives of ministry in the process. From the start she stretches the ministerial intellect and shifts the traditional paradigm. No matter how successful your ministry has been or how long you've been in the pastorate, after you read this book you can't help but ask, "Lord, what's next?"

—DANIEL CRUZ
PRESIDENT, FAITHWORLD INTERNATIONAL MINISTRIES

This book does not belong in your library. It belongs on your desktop! Whether you lead a ministry or run a business, your pathway to legacy will become clearer as you read this book. Anchored by her experiences in building and leading a global ministry, Naomi Dowdy delivers page after page of practical principles that fit any type of organization. If longevity is your goal, you need to start reading this book today!

—MARK PFEIFER, MARK AND NICKI PFEIFER MINISTRIES

Thank you for another just-in-time book in the Moving On and Moving Up series. As ever, it is not easy to misunderstand your teaching, and the practical illustrations are always helpful. Please accept a personal "thank you" for your insights and practical wisdom. After only a few weeks, I have started to make plans for future ministry developments.

—ALAN WHARTON
STRATEGIC MINISTER/CONSULTANT AND TRAINER
UNITED REFORMED CHURCH, UK

Many leaders hold on to a ministry beyond the time of effectiveness because they are uncertain of the steps for transition. Dr. Naomi Dowdy provides life experience, practical application, prophetic insight, and apostolic challenge to propel individuals forward. We have benefitted greatly in our ministry by applying the spiritual truths of legacy management and intentional transition. We challenge you to read and apply the truths found in these pages and shift into your new day.

—RENEE DUNCAN
DIRECTOR, ALASKA WOMEN UNLIMITED A/G
CO-PASTOR, PENINSULA CHRISTIAN CENTER
JAMES DUNCAN
SECRETARY, ALASKA MINISTRY NETWORK
PASTOR, PENINSULA CHRISTIAN CENTER

Moving On
and Moving Up
from Succession to Significance

Practical Principles for Legacy
Management & Leadership Transition

Naomi Dowdy

CREATION HOUSE
A STRANG COMPANY

MOVING ON AND MOVING UP FROM SUCCESSION TO
SIGNIFICANCE by Naomi Dowdy
Published by Creation House
A Strang Company
600 Rinehart Road
Lake Mary, Florida 32746
www.strangbookgroup.com

Unless otherwise marked, all Scripture quotations
marked NIV are from the Holy Bible, New International
Version of the Bible. Copyright © 1973, 1978, 1984,
International Bible Society. Used by permission.

Cover Design by River Design (Singapore)
Strang Communications Design Director: Bill Johnson

Library of Congress Control Number: 2010937178
International Standard Book Number: 978-1-61638-262-9
E-book ISBN: 978-1-61638-365-7

First Edition

10 11 12 13 14 — 9 8 7 6 5 4 3 2 1
Printed in the United States of America

Contents

Introduction 1

Chapter 1
Where It Began.. 5

Chapter 2
Don't Limit Your Tomorrows............................... 13

Chapter 3
Finding a Better Way.. 21

Chapter 4
Understanding Biblical Succession 29

Chapter 5
The Call to Leadership.. 39

Chapter 6
Leadership Transition Begins with Leadership
Development.. 47

Chapter 7
Identifying Potential Successors 59

Chapter 8
Coaching Your Leadership Team 71

Chapter 9
Choices Determine Destiny 81

Chapter 10
Transition Is a Process 89

Chapter 11
Pitfalls to Avoid 101

Chapter 12
Time for Handover 109

Chapter 13
Change of Command 117

Chapter 14
Waking Up to a New Day 121

Epilogue
Your Next Level: Significance 131

Introduction

THE MOMENT YOU TAKE THE leadership of a church, a ministry, a company, or any kind of organization, your goal should be the raising of a successor who will continue your work and advance the cause further than you have.

Unfortunately, leadership development and succession rank low on the list of priorities for most busy leaders. We are more likely to be consumed by the urgent day-to-day tasks at hand.

Most of us have not paused long enough to ask ourselves a very pointed question: "What will I do after I am no longer the CEO, the managing director, or the senior pastor?" Instead, we think, "I am just getting started. Anyway, if I did hand it over to someone else, what would I *do*?"

Consider this: God called you, and God put His gifts and anointing upon your life. Therefore, God's calling and gifts are in *you*, not in your title. Regardless of a title or no title, with a church or no church, with a company or no company, God's gifts are still in you.

That being true, then the better question to ask is this: "What will be the 'expression' of God's gift through me during my next season, when I no longer have my present title?" When you can settle this in your spirit, you will eliminate the fear of what's next. You do not want to quit. You still want to be involved.

Do not sell yourself short: *God has more for you than what you are currently doing.* So if you want to move on and move up in God—and do what is truly best for both you and your organization—you have to start the process of leadership transition from day one.

Planning for succession does not necessarily mean that you would not continue doing what you love, or what God has designed and gifted you to do. If you have discovered your gift, passion, and anointing, it's more likely than not that you will use that gift. However, it may be in a different expression or in a larger capacity.

The divine assignments God gives us are often really stepping-stones to the greater things He has in store for us. But if we cannot let go of the present and imagine a future beyond what we are currently doing, we will never be able to receive the new things that God has in store for us, nor envision a dramatically different future.

This Can't Be It

In my book *Moving On and Moving Up: 10 Practical Principles for Getting to the Next Level*, I mentioned that everywhere I looked as I traveled the globe, I saw God moving His people to the next level.

He is moving us forward in our destinies, advancing us in His purposes, and equipping us for greater accomplishments than we have ever known. He is doing this so his Kingdom can be established and increased in each sphere of every society on Earth.

God is always doing new things, and though we may be content where we are right now, it is unlikely that in His plans, you and I are to do exactly what we are presently doing until God calls us home. God has promised, "the latter glory of this house will be greater than the former" (Haggai 2:9, NAS).

Like the apostle Paul who said, "...not that I have already arrived, but I press on toward the high calling in God," (author's paraphrase) I can say I definitely do not have all the answers concerning God's new way of making transitions. However, I have learned a lot about the process of leadership transition, and this journey has enabled me to help many others.

Speaking from my position as the former senior pastor of Trinity Christian Centre, I attest to a successful leadership transition. But this did not happen naturally or accidentally. There are factors in the leadership transition process I designed to facilitate a smooth handover; one that positioned everyone involved for greater things as they moved on and moved up in God.

Whether you are leading a church, a para-church ministry, or a business, the principles in this book will apply to you if you are seeking kingdom principles relating to leadership development and transition.

It is my prayer that this book, and the illustration of my journey in Trinity Christian Centre, will now help you move toward a successful transition. I will also share some important elements regarding your significance and legacy. If you need further help, just give me a call or send me an e-mail at info@naomidowdy.com. With God's enablement, I am here to serve you.

Your Partner in a Journey,

Naomi Dowdy
www.naomidowdy.com

CHAPTER 1

Where It Began
A Place of Destiny

I FIRST VISITED SINGAPORE IN 1972. I was invited to return in 1975 to meet with a denominational leadership team and plan for meetings in the nation during the following years.

Through a series of events, I discovered that a small pioneering church was losing their current pastor (due to some immigration and visa issues, which later turned out to be a case of mistaken identity). It was a church of young, eager believers. Yet, in a span of five years, as a pioneer church, they had gone through the transition of three pastors.

It was during this discovery that God spoke to me: "You are to pastor this church." This was one of those "audible voice" experiences. "But God," I said, "I am not interested in becoming a pastor. I am an evangelist and I love it!" To me, pastoring was not my gift.

This small church had baptized their first forty-two members and elected their very first board. Their first board meeting was to decide what to do about the loss of their pastor. They had no guidance, no experience, and no training in such matters. Naturally they were concerned about the future and what to do as a church.

That inaugural board and the leadership of the

denomination invited me to become their pastor. I only later discovered the truth; no one wanted to become the pastor. Other leaders did not want to handle the internal problems that existed. Things were not looking good. Besides the internal problems, they were concerned they could not pay their bills, and they retreated from meeting in a hotel ballroom to a small residential location. I joked that it was a church of forty-two members and seventy-five problems.

For me, it was an intense time of wrestling with God. Needless to say, I lost my wrestling match with God and eventually accepted their request to take up the position as the new senior pastor for six months, which was later extended to a year. During this time, I told them, "Please keep looking for a pastor, as I am only here for a season—while you find the right person."

That church was Trinity Christian Centre (TCC) in Singapore. Today, I can jokingly say that my "interim" season lasted almost thirty years!

Discovering Why

In reality, God had positioned me for a major transition. Prior to this, He had been dealing with me about

I joked that it was a church of forty-two members and seventy-five problems.

changes that needed to take place in local churches and in our methods of evangelism. Thus, as we began to see the church turn around and begin growing, God made it clear why I was to become a pastor. He wanted me to

6

lead a local church in order to create a "new model" for churches in several areas. You cannot create God's new model unless you are actually "doing" the new things He is saying.

Suddenly, I knew it was time to integrate the things God had been dealing with me about concerning the church. Clearly, He had spoken to me about change and the church—what the church should be and how the church should function. I was no longer focused on leaving. God had changed my heart; I loved pastoring and I loved the people. People were coming to Christ, miracles were happening, and the spirit in the church was being completely transformed. The congregation grew and became focused on changing lives and impacting the nation.

However, even in those early years, God began prompting me to increase the number of preachers in the church. He was directing me not to be the only preacher every Sunday, nor to have someone else preach

In reality, God had positioned me for a major transition.

only when I was not around. He was saying, "It is not good that the church is growing on your pulpit ministry. It is time to change." God prompted me to begin training a "preaching team." This launched us into a whole new phase of development within the church.

Beyond Recognition

Through the next thirty years, God was faithful—through many ups and downs—and by God's grace:

- **Trinity Christian Centre grew in size**, from forty-two members to 4,600 in attendance at the time of transition.
- **The church grew in vision**, from a group of young believers to mature leaders in a national and global church.
- **The church effectively multiplied its leadership base**, from a handful of leaders to approximately 1,000 lay leaders and spiritual parents.
- **It had a powerful music and drama ministry**, which staged many performances that had a lasting impact on lives across denominational lines. It staged the first *Singing Christmas Tree* on Orchard Road, Singapore's main shopping street in 1982, which became a national attraction every Christmas.
- **It enlarged people's vision** of what Children's Ministry really should be: kids with kingdom hearts and kingdom principles of living and giving.
- **It broke into the airwaves**, with a daily devotional program that could be heard in Singapore and in other parts of the region.
- **It grew in space**, with three properties in Singapore, and all on freehold land, in a city where land is scarce and most church properties are on thirty-year lease land.

- **It had developed a powerful small group ministry** called Carecells. This ministry spanned all age groups from children to adults. It touched youth on every major college campus in the nation and had a ministry to military personnel.
- **It had an apostolic leadership role** and a voice in the nation of Singapore.
- **It became a global voice** in the Christian world.
- **It expanded into new arenas of influence,** far beyond that of a normal local church—through TCA College, Care Community Services Society, Global Leadership Network, Global Business Network Partners and Global Covenant Network—each of these became its own "organization."
- **It developed a world-impacting missions outreach**.
- **It raised prophetic intercessors**, prophets with a powerful anointing, plus emerging apostles with kingdom strategies. During these years, my goal was always to raise leaders in Singapore who would not only impact their own nation but also be able to impact other nations.
- **I had multiplied myself**, expanding the pastoral team from one (me) to forty-five pastors. More than 90 percent of these pastors were homegrown, and they were all anointed and gifted.

Do It Right

As you can tell, it took time to arrive at the juncture for transition. It was a journey. It took years, and there was much work to get done. It was not something that could just happen overnight. The desire was there, the purpose was there, but there needed to be an internal process within the church structure that could develop every believer into a kingdom-minded leader. We did not reach this historic milestone by accident; I had to develop an intentional leadership development process.

Leadership transition is a journey and will take several years of groundwork. Now you can understand why I say you should begin from day one. If you can, it is advisable to allow at least five to eight years for the process.

I know many of you will not have the luxury of that much time. You did not begin preparing soon enough, thus you now find yourself pressured to make the transition as soon as possible. This is when you need to call in someone who understands the dynamics of transition to assist you, someone who can help guide you through an accelerated transition plan. I will talk more about this journey in another chapter.

Successful Succession

After many years, through the process of intentional leadership development, all the pieces were in place and the timing was right. I had found the right person to become the senior pastor of Trinity Christian Centre, and he was *now* ready to lead the church onward into her prophetic destiny.

On March 10, 2005, we had a "Change of Command" service and commissioned Rev. Dominic Yeo to be the new senior pastor of the church. God had promised that the "latter glory of this church would be greater than the former." I released and claimed that Word.

I was confident that under his leadership, working with all the other excellent staff and leaders in the church, Trinity Christian Centre would experience the best years and finest hour of her ministry.

We did not reach this historic milestone by accident.

To date, it can be said that the handover to my successor has been successful—not perfect, but successful. Under the capable and anointed leadership of Rev. Dominic Yeo, Trinity Christian Centre has continued to grow in every aspect. It has grown numerically, financially, and spiritually. In fact, the church—not only the senior pastor, but the pastoral team, leaders, and congregation—is moving on and moving up in God.

God has kept His promise. Not only are we seeing greater glory in the house, but also the journey we have undertaken has now become a model for others to follow.

CHAPTER 2

Don't Limit Your Tomorrows

M OST PASTORS AND LEADERS I know love their work and have never really paused long enough to seriously consider an actual succession plan. Sure, they know it must happen some day, but it is not something they feel an urgency to plan for at this present time. In their minds, there is still so much more they want to do, so many new things they want to see happen, and they can't imagine the day when they will no longer be doing this kind of thinking and planning. They still want to initiate so many new things and expand in so many new areas. Does that sound like *you?*

We can't assume that we will always be in the same leadership role we are in right now. We live in a world of rapid, drastic, and sometimes disorientating change. What happens when you are no longer able to function the way you do right now—because of health, family, or other issues? What are the implications? A responsible leader will plan for the future of the organization beyond his/her tenure—and build a team of leaders *and* a successor who will continue God's work after his/her exit.

For this reason, you must start planning and preparing for your successor *from day one.*

The Best Person for the Job Is...

Many leaders are tempted to try and do it all alone. Oh, we have assistants to help us, and we appoint this committee and that committee, but deep down, we believe that we are the best person for the job, and that no one else can do it better than we can. Some leaders can even develop what is called a "Messiah" complex. This is a subtle thinking that goes like this: "The church and the people cannot do it without me."

We can't assume that we will always be in the same leadership role we are in now.

You may even think to yourself, "I *am* mentoring my staff." You would even tell others, "Yes, I am developing leaders." Yet, after years of such activity, deep inside you know none of them are actually *ready* to take on your role in the church or business.

In reality you have just been fooling yourself. This can happen for several reasons:

- **You do not really *want* them to be** good enough to take your place.
- **You have hired and surrounded yourself with people who are good followers** whom you feel will be loyal and "safe." They would never rise up to become a threat to you or try to assume your position.

- **You have not taken time to even consider that you will need to *pass the baton*** at some stage. It is always something slated for the far distant future.
- **You were not mentored personally** and thus you really do not know *how* to mentor a successor.
- **You are only focused on the here and now**, and have not made longer-term plans—whether for yourself or for the organization. Procrastination, ego, and pride can play a big role in our failure to plan soon enough for transition.

As Dwight Eisenhower said, "The important is seldom urgent and the urgent is seldom important."

Your Latter Can Be Greater

Do you really want to do what you are doing now *for the rest of your life?* Even if you love what you do, who is to say that God won't call you to a bigger role or larger capacity?

Daniel 2:21 teaches us that God is a God of change, and He will reposition us for the times and seasons He has prepared for our lives. He is always moving us from glory to glory, preparing us to be used in new and different ways for the days ahead. God is always shifting people from one assignment to the next, from one sphere of influence to the next, from one opportu-

> *God is always shifting people from one assignment to the next.*

nity to the next, and now, from one season to the next. That's just what He does!

He declares, "Forget the things that happened in the past. Do not keep thinking about them. I am about to do something new. It is beginning to happen *even now*. Don't you see it coming?" (Isaiah 43:18–19, NIV, emphasis added)

Have you stopped to consider that God has a new season for His Kingdom and for your life? God *does* have new assignments for His present leaders. He has dreams for your tomorrows that you have yet to perceive. It is these new possibilities that I want to see explode in your spirit. In order for these possibilities to become realities, you need to make some transitions *now*. If you don't, you won't be in position when God calls you to step into His next season for your life.

> *God has dreams for your tomorrows that you have yet to perceive.*

Each role God has given us must be seen as contributing to the overall development of who we are in God. Each event in life and ministry is part of God's school to mold and shape us for later stages in our life.

Consider this: Perhaps everything you have been doing up until this present moment was actually practice and preparation for your *real* assignment from God. Could it be that your finest hour is yet ahead? What is God speaking to you about moving on and moving up?

Old Words Can Limit Us

There have been many expressions spoken by pastors and leaders in the past that became the epitome of complete devotion to God. Even I caught those expressions and often repeated them. Some of you will remember hearing things like: "I will do this till the very end," "I want to die preaching in the pulpit," or "I am not retired, I am re-fired."

People would cheer such remarks and cheer the person making them, even though they were so physically weak they needed to be helped across the room. Without realizing it, this language and environment created a mindset in leaders that they should never consider "passing the baton" to new leaders: "You must hang onto your position until you die; you do not quit. It is not spiritual to stop."

I experienced this myself. When I was young in the ministry, these phrases stuck in my mind and spirit. "Yes, this is the way to go. You must be totally sold out for God. Never stop, never slow down." Without knowing it, it could also mean never stepping aside to give someone else a chance to rise up.

Don't Be the Bottleneck

Here is a fact to remember: those serving under you cannot rise to a higher level until you get out of the way. Thus in reality, you can become the "bottleneck" to progress in your church or your organization. Sorry, but this is an organizational reality.

Think about it, it is all about timing. Admit it, timing is a big issue. Some people think that a person in his sixties is old. But the person at age sixty may still be thinking like a thirty- or forty-year-old, trapped inside a sixty-year-old body.

Listen, just because your desires are still there and your mind is still active, it does not necessarily mean you should stay put in your present position. Don't become a bottleneck to what God wants to accomplish.

Is it possible that our message and leadership style can become outdated for this present season? Deep in our heart we want to see things turn around, but regardless of

Those serving "under" you cannot rise to a higher level until you get out of the way.

what we do, things keep slipping downhill. This can also be a sign that it is time to pass the baton.

King David had to face this reality. He wanted to build a temple for God, but he was not the person to do the building. Yes, he had the desire. He was active to promote its building. He diligently gathered the resources to ensure it could be done. However, with all of that burning within his heart, he had to admit, "I am not the one who will do the building."

In David's case, God had selected his son Solomon for the honor of building the new temple for the Lord. In case you did not realize it, this must have been hard for David. He wanted to do it. It was his dream, his vision, and his passion. But the reality was, "David, you are not the man for the job. God has chosen someone else. Can you accept that and pass the baton over to him? Now move on and let him do the building!"

Legacy Management

Leaving a legacy is an important issue I feel we often overlook. You have worked hard to pastor the church and lead the organization. You have given your time, your energy, your finances, and really, your life for the work of God. If you did not raise and develop spiritual sons and daughters who share your vision, know your heart, have grown with the church or organization, and leaders who understand the challenges of the people and their families, what can happen?

I can tell you what usually happens. As soon as you leave and transition out of the church or organization, a new leader will come in and "tear down" everything you have worked and sacrificed for and rebuild it from scratch, according to his/her personal vision. That is going to be hard for you and for the people. It can almost become years of wasted time, energy, money, and calling.

The above scenario is both hurtful and wasteful. Every one of us wants to feel that God is pleased with our efforts and to hear Him say, "Well done, good and faithful servant." Friends, you don't want to have started well in ministry and then not finish well. How you transition will determine if you really do finish well.

How you transition will determine if you really do finish well.

By God's grace you have built something over the years. Whatever God has used you to build, you do not want to see it crumble. Rather, you should desire to see the fruit of your labor withstand the test of time—to continue to grow and fulfill God's destiny. You want your life's work to become a legacy of God's faithfulness. The only way to ensure that is to be intentional about leadership succession. As it has been said, "There is no success without a successor."

Now is the time for you to leave a legacy. How? By shifting from success to significance! Therefore, the challenge before us is to consider a better way of transitioning from one leader to another—by *leaving a legacy.*

CHAPTER 3

Finding a Better Way

T HROUGH THE CENTURIES, CHURCHES HAVE transitioned from one pastor to another and from one leader to another. Sometimes it has worked well, but more often it has not.

This centuries-old process, which is still being used by most churches, places the responsibility of searching for a new senior pastor on their elected church board, who are lay leaders that give freely of their time to serve the church.

Personally, I have strong feelings about this process that places such a heavy responsibility onto these wonderful men and women without any real help or guidance. I believe more in the selection and appointment of a new senior pastor rather than a congregational election. The selection of spiritual leaders should be done by senior leadership that is called, anointed, and has the experience to walk through this important process. Naturally, the board should have the power to *affirm* who the new senior pastor will be.

All too often, their selection of the new pastor is based upon hearing a sample of the candidate's preaching and a brief interview. The results are based more upon "feeling" and brief impressions rather than a God-called, God-sent, God-selected leader for the next phase of the church.

Regardless of the prayer, time, and energy that are poured into this process, it does not ensure there will be a "match" in vision, goals, and values between the new senior pastor and the existing church.

This process usually results in one of three things happening.

A Transitional Pastor

The first scenario is that the new pastor ends up becoming what we call a "transitional" pastor; someone who comes in and leads the church for a short period of time. Perhaps it could be because the board could not find a suitable candidate; they choose someone and hope that somehow things might work out. But after the person takes on the role, they realize that it was simply not a good fit for the long term.

In such a situation, the appointed pastor takes on all the responsibilities of getting to know the congregation and helping the church through the many adjustments required, only to discover that their tenure will last only three years or less.

This throws the church back into the whole process of finding another new pastor all over again. They must now begin looking for a more suitable person to become the senior pastor. This will result in yet another transition and more adjustments for every level of leadership in the church and the entire congregation. There are several large and mega churches that I could name that have experienced this in their transitions.

A Maintenance Pastor

A second scenario is that the new pastor ends up becoming what I call a "maintenance" pastor; someone who comes in to lead the church but who has no real influence to make significant changes. The lay leaders have such great power that the pastor is reduced to being a hireling.

Since the pastor can only make minor or cosmetic changes to the church, he operates in maintenance mode. In other words, he operates within a system or a culture that is so entrenched that *he* has to conform to it, instead of bringing change that will take the church forward into a new level in God.

This means the church does not move on and move up. It is stuck in its old ways and mindsets; it never breaks through into new levels of growth and glory; it does not fulfill its kingdom potential. This is the sad reality for many churches today.

All-out Change

In the third scenario, the new pastor who comes from outside the church wants to release all the present staff and bring in all new staff—people from elsewhere whom they know or have relationships with. Since the new pastor does not know the people and does not have relationships with the existing leadership, he prefers to bring in his own team from outside the organization. This becomes a huge adjustment for the stakeholders in the church or organization.

Now, the whole church has the trauma of a total shift in relationships. They must now build relationships with all or almost all new leaders. When this happens there will usually be major changes in other areas as well. With new leadership, there will usually be a change in vision, introduction of new values, programs, and ideas. Suddenly, everything is "out the window," because a new pharaoh has arisen in the land.

In reality, the new leader should be able to continue growing and building upon what God has already done in the church or organization, rather than lose valuable kingdom time by "tearing down" what is already there, and then embarking on a long process of trying to rebuild the organization from top to bottom according to his/her personal vision. The new leader should be building upon the foundations already laid, rather than rebuilding them.

Not Homegrown

What do these diverse scenarios have in common? In each of these scenarios, someone was brought in from outside the organization to lead it. He or she is not a spiritual son or daughter of the house. In other words, the new leader is not *homegrown*.

When we fail to develop homegrown leaders, there will always be a big relationship gap. It is like a couple that decides to get married first, and then begins to date so they can get to know each other.

The tragedy is this: all of the years of prayer, tears, sacrifice, relationship-building, money, and work that had already gone into the church are now completely wiped off the landscape. Sure, there may be a building and some people, but what happens to all the things you worked hard to see achieved? Where are they now? *Where is your legacy?* This accepted process has indeed cost the kingdom of God dearly. This makes me wonder: why do we continue to allow this tragedy to happen?

In Search of a Model

During the years when I was preparing for my own transition, I looked for possible models of the transition process, but I could not find any acceptable models for us to learn from or follow in our journey of transition. Yes, there were pastors who left their churches and gave the leadership over to a new pastor, but none of them fit into what I considered to be a strong model we could follow. I talked to other leaders; I tried searching for books that might help us, but I could not find anything that could serve as a model. It became very clear that God wanted us to create or establish a new model that could serve other pastors and churches in the future.

> *In reality, the new leader should be able to continue building upon what God has already done in the church or organization.*

I prayed over this for many nights, asking God for revelation concerning my transition out of Trinity Christian Centre. I knew that this would not just be for

Trinity, but would become a model for other churches and leaders to follow. There was an awesome sense of responsibility that I felt on my shoulders during that time.

Singapore as a Nation

As I prayed and thought further, I realized that through the years Trinity was functioning with somewhat the same philosophy as the nation of Singapore. Singapore as a nation was closer to our journey than anything else.

On the political front, Singapore's former prime minister (now minister mentor) Lee Kuan Yew had modeled for the world an effective transition of leadership. He did not wait until he was voted out of his position or until he was ready to retire. While he was in office, despite being able to function in his role, he selected from among his team those who might become his successor. He mentored these persons and stepped down *while* he was still in his elected term, so that his successor could step in to serve out the remainder of his term.

It became very clear that God wanted us to create or establish a new model that could serve others in the future.

He also had no model. He is the only governmental leader in the world to have implemented such a succession plan. There was preparation, selection, mentoring, affirmation and the handover—all the ingredients of a successful succession.

This was a very wise and bold step on his part as a leader. He himself stayed on in the newly created role of senior minister, and then later as minister mentor. He availed his wisdom and counsel to the cabinet, but made it clear that the decisions were theirs to make. He has established an effective model that works and which ensures the ongoing growth, vision, and development of this nation.

Apostle Paul

In a way, the apostle Paul became somewhat of a model for us because his ministry was local, regional, and global. First of all, wherever Paul ministered, he instilled a vision within the local church for what we today would call missions. Secondly, he was always raising leaders in each local church. He would spend time preaching and teaching in those locations, often for up to two years.

The apostle Paul did not stop there. In his travels, he would return to those churches to further train them and upgrade them in their understanding of how to deal with problems in the local church. In other words, he continued to mentor and disciple them in their role as leaders. They did not use the title pastor as we do today; however, they were identified as the spiritual leaders of the church.

Paul's training was structured to take them from pre-believers, see them come to that place of receiving Jesus Christ as Lord and Savior, and then through more training, see these new converts become leaders in their spheres.

It was *intentional* and *homegrown* leadership development. This is a key to successful succession.

CHAPTER 4

Understanding Biblical Succession
The Way God Designed It

GOD-ORDAINED AND GOD-LED LEADERSHIP transition is something we see in Scripture, and here are some models for us to learn from and follow.

Moses to Joshua

> So the LORD said to Moses, "Take Joshua son of Nun, a man in whom is the spirit, and lay your hand on him. Have him stand before Eleazar the priest and the entire assembly and commission him in their presence. *Give him some of your authority* so the whole Israelite community will obey him." Moses did as the LORD commanded him. He took Joshua and had him stand before Eleazar the priest and the whole assembly. Then he laid his hands on him and commissioned him, as the LORD instructed through Moses.
> —NUMBERS 27:18–20, 22–23, EMPHASIS ADDED

If you follow the life of Joshua, you will find that he served Moses for nearly forty years. He was an understudy who was mentored and trained for a greater leadership role.

Notice some of the qualities that God highlighted in choosing Joshua:

- Joshua was a man of prayer. He would linger in the presence of God even after Moses had left the place of prayer.
- He was a man who manifested the indwelling presence of the Holy Spirit.
- Joshua and Moses fought battles together as a team. Moses' role was to stand on the mountain with uplifted arms, even getting some help from Aaron and Hur, while Joshua was in the valley swinging his sword. But each had their role in the battle, and together they were a winning team.

When the time came for Joshua to take on the leadership role, God desired to release an even greater anointing into his life because of the new level of responsibility he would be carrying. How did God say this would happen? There would be a transfer as the present leader (Moses) gives and releases some of his higher-level anointing and authority into the new leader's life.

The same thing should be happening today. The next generation of leaders after you should be able to stand on your shoulders, so to speak, and build from that vantage point. They should not go back and start all over from ground zero, taking years to get back to the place where you left off.

There should be a transfer of trust, respect, and confidence—relational capital, if you like—that is passed on to, and inherited by, the new and younger leader. The veteran leader positions the younger one, by way of association and affirmation. This association of an older minister standing with the younger one will drastically shorten the time needed for the younger one to build a reputation of his/her own. This will thus accelerate the work and development of the church or organization and the kingdom of God. I will share more about this in another chapter.

Elijah to Elisha

> When they had crossed, Elijah said to Elisha, "Tell me, what can I do for you before I am taken from you?" "Let me inherit a double portion of your spirit," Elisha replied. "You have asked a difficult thing," Elijah said, "yet if you see me when I am taken from you, it will be yours—otherwise not." As they were walking along and talking together, suddenly a chariot of fire and horses of fire appeared and separated the two of them, and Elijah went up to heaven in a whirlwind...[Elisha] picked up the cloak that had fallen from Elijah... The company of the prophets from Jericho, who were watching, said, *"The spirit of Elijah is resting on Elisha."*
> —2 KINGS 2:9–11, 13, 15, EMPHASIS ADDED

In the lives of Elijah and Elisha, we see that there was a transfer of two things:

- The Transfer of **Leadership**—resulting in the *Recognition of New Leadership*
- The Transfer of **Anointing**—resulting in the *Release of New Anointing*

I believe you should always see these two dimensions involved in the transition of leaders. When leadership transition takes place, it is not merely an official or ceremonial handover; there should also be a shift that takes place in the heavens.

There should be an impartation so there will be increased anointing on the new leader's life and ministry. Elisha's anointing enabled him to see double the

> *The next generation of leaders after you should be able to stand on your shoulders, so to speak, and build from that vantage point.*

number of miracles that Elijah saw during his ministry. He moved on and moved up beyond what Elijah had accomplished during his watch. This is an incredible testimony of God's calling and the transfer or impartation of power.

Both Joshua and Elisha moved from ministering in the shadow of someone else's ministry, in the wings of the stage, to the prime position as the leader. Neither of them is seen struggling or striving for a leadership position. They each served their mentor with a learning posture. They wanted to be ready for God's timing and appointment. Neither of them was restless while serving and waiting for God's timing. Both of them displayed the highest integrity in honor of their mentor.

32

When the appointed time for transition took place, both Joshua and Elisha immediately demonstrated a higher level of anointing. *When* did this happen? *After* the transfer of leadership.

Moses had laid the groundwork for Joshua. Moses had developed and established the Jewish people from being slaves into a people of God. Moses had to take a people "who were not a people" and forge them into a people of God. He had to lead a group of downtrodden slaves, made up of several tribes, to form one nation with a strong national identity. It was a time of transformation.

Looking at their giftings, we could infer that Moses was more pastoral and Joshua was more apostolic. Joshua was a warrior leader, the kind of leader needed to take the people forward into a time of conquest. His assignment was different and required a different anointing. Joshua was a leader for a time of war and the conquest of new territory. The nation needed a new leadership style in order to go in and claim their inheritance.

When leadership transition takes place, there should also be a shift that takes place in the heavens.

Peter to James

The book of Acts begins with the outpouring of the Holy Spirit. There were 120 disciples gathered in the upper room. Upon receiving God's gift, manifested by tongues of fire appearing over them, these empowered disciples moved out of that upper room and spilled into the streets of Jerusalem. When people began to question what was happening, Peter began to speak and explain. We see that Peter was the acknowledged leader of this first group of believers.

When did Joshua and Elisha demonstrate a higher level of anointing? After the transfer of leadership.

By the time we read about the council in Jerusalem in Acts 15, we see that James was the new apostle and leader of the church in that city. The Scripture does not tell us when the transition took place nor how it took place.

Nonetheless, by Acts 15, everyone, including Peter, recognized James as the new apostle in Jerusalem. There must have been a smooth transition, as Scripture does not record for us that it was an unpleasant event.

Jesus to His Disciples

Let's look at the model of Jesus. He took a band of men who were mostly unschooled and came from the fringe of society. He called them, discipled, and mentored them. When the timing was right, as recorded in Mark 3:14 and Luke 6:13, He called them and designated them apostles. Then when his time had come, he passed the commission the Father gave Him onto this band of disciples. He told them, "As the Father has sent me, I am sending you" (John 20:21).

Looking at Scripture, we can see that Jesus was planning for succession from day one. Jesus was intentional in His succession plan. Over a period of three years, Jesus prepared for leadership transition. He was keenly aware of the fact that He would not be with His disciples for long. He was deliberate in building a team of apostles who would carry on and perpetuate His vision of God's kingdom.

When Jesus' transition was complete, He moved from the success of His mission into His new season of greater significance. He moved on and moved up into a new season and into new expressions of His ministry.

I believe that God wants you to be just as strategic and intentional in your life and ministry. Do not assume that you will always be in your present leadership position. You are there only for a season. You have but a window of opportunity. While the window is still open to you, how will you build? What will your legacy be? How will you perpetuate it?

> *When Jesus' transition was complete, He moved from the success of His mission into His new season of greater significance.*

The Great Omission

Clearly, one of the responsibilities of a leader is to raise new leaders, and to pass the baton properly to the next leader. Unfortunately most Christian organizations and churches have failed to raise spiritual sons and daughters and to prepare them for a transition of leadership. This is a tragedy.

Some have passed the ministries or organizations

over to their natural son or daughter, who may or may not have the same mantle of anointing as their parents. In some cases, it has been like the sons of Eli, where his children did not carry "the father's anointing." In other cases, it was a process of election. The election resulted in the appointment of someone "safe" who would carry on doing what was originally envisioned—someone who would not "rock the boat."

As a result, these once cutting-edge ministries have now been placed into the hands of "administrative leadership." The apostolic anointing that once birthed those ministries is no longer evident in the next generation.

You may ask, "Should there be another apostolic anointing that would follow the original birthing anointing?" Yes! The apostle Paul stirred up an anointing within a young man named Timothy. He then instructed Timothy to continue the mentoring process (2 Tim. 2:2).

> *Unfortunately, most Christian organizations and churches have failed to raise spiritual sons and daughters.*

You can see from Scripture that young Timothy seemed to have more of a pastoral anointing in his earlier years of ministry. However, later we see Paul sending Timothy to function in the role and anointing of an apostle. Thus we can see that Paul mentored Timothy in his spiritual gifts and expected him to grow in God's anointing. This process opened the door for an even greater anointing to develop within Timothy so his function within the body of Christ could increase in responsibility.

Listen, powerful churches, ministries, and organizations cannot advance under administrative leadership. They require leaders who have an apostolic and prophetic anointing. We must have men and women who have an ear to hear what the Spirit is saying for each of God's new seasons—leaders who will receive God's progressive revelation and lead us forward into new levels of breakthrough.

Both churches and businesses functioning in today's world must deal with increasingly complex issues—and there are greater challenges looming ahead for both spheres. Thus in order to see the fulfillment of God's promises to us, today's leaders must be persons of prayer who are able to hear the voice of God.

> *Powerful churches, ministries, and organizations cannot advance under administrative leadership.*

In the shifting sands of today's society, the leader must be someone who hears God's voice and discerns the times and seasons. Like the sons of Issachar, they must understand the times and the seasons, and know what Israel should do (1 Chron. 12:32).

Chapter 5

The Call to Leadership
What It's All About

EVERYWHERE I GO AS I travel the globe, I see an impending disaster looming over churches, denominations, and para-church organizations, and even in many businesses in the marketplace: there is a lack of leadership to take these organizations and kingdom businesses forward into God's new seasons.

At this point, I must make a clear distinction between leadership and management. Too often, when people graduate from Bible school or seminary, they think, "Oh, I'm a leader. I can lead a church now." Sorry, that degree doesn't automatically make you a leader. This is where we have constantly made a grave mistake.

We have *assumed* people would be leaders, just because they had a degree. So we put them into positions of leadership, expecting leadership results. These are unreal expectations that we put on them, because we have not mentored them, and we have not trained them yet.

Yes, we have given them an education *about* leadership but we have not engaged them in the hands-on experience necessary to develop the natural and spiritual skills necessary to function as a leader. We have not equipped them nor prepared them for the *actual*, day-to-day functions of leadership. Yes, you can always look for "born" leaders whom you can poach from someone else. But even those who seem to be born leaders need to develop the full potential of their God-given gift. It is more than just head knowledge but the combination of head knowledge with "real" challenges, with real people in a variety of situations. These are the opportunities for real leaders to emerge.

In Bible schools and seminaries through the years, at least in the last generation, we have been very successful at producing managers but we have failed in producing leaders. We produce men and women who think like managers and who *lead* like managers.

Don't get me wrong; we definitely need managers in our churches and organizations, but having managers without true leaders results in a people focused on maintaining the status quo. These managers are good people, but their anointing and gifts are not what is needed to take the church or organization forward into God's new seasons. They cannot break out of the loop. They cannot break out of the ordinary. Managers are leaders in their own right—but within parameters.

> *There is a lack of leadership to take these organizations and kingdom businesses forward into God's new seasons.*

Leaders—God's Change Agents

Leaders are those who hear from God and, as a result, set new parameters, push back frontiers, and pioneer new models of ministry. Leaders provide the ideas, the strategy and the motivation for effective ministry and organizations. Managers design the structures, systems, and tactics that implement the vision conveyed by the leader. They complement each other.

While it has been relatively easy to define the work of managers, both business and church organizations have come to realize that a clear understanding of leadership has been elusive. Leadership is hard to define, but there are some characteristics that are common to all leaders, which enable them to take their organizations forward into God's new seasons.

- Leaders communicate a **vision**.
- Leaders have the ability to **make things happen** (action).
- Leaders realize that **prayer is not a substitute for action**. You have shifted from leader-led to committee-led when you hear over and over again, "Let's pray about it, let's defer it to the next meeting, let's assign it to a committee for study." Those are the words of a "committee mentality," not a leader.
- Leaders have the ability to make **swift and clear decisions**. That means being decisive, and taking responsibility for the decisions they make.
- Leaders are **men and women of faith**. In my opinion, to be a leader and not have faith is almost contradictory because leaders are risk-takers. Leaders have to step out when others are holding back. Whether they are Christians or not, there is a "faith" (risk-taking) element needed. When they have to step out of the boat, they have to dare to

take the leap of faith. (The key is making sure you have heard from God.)

■ Leaders **inspire** and motivate the organization.

Because we have produced managers—instead of leaders—through the years, we are now stuck with many pastors who are unknowingly serving with a management mentality. Yet, we are expecting them to function as leaders within our churches and organizations.

With this cycle continuing for so many years, it has now resulted in scores of pastors who are reaching an age where leadership transition needs to take place,

Leaders are those who hear from God and, as a result, set new parameters, push back frontiers, and pioneer new models of ministry.

but they have not developed the leaders necessary for this critical juncture in history. As a result, leadership transition has become a critical issue everywhere.

No Instant Leadership Development

Listen, we cannot just pack our emerging leaders off to a Bible school and, upon their return, expect them to start functioning as a leader and leading the church. There is a *process* of leadership development that must take place. Leadership is a learned behavior. It is learned through a process, which includes mentoring, exposure, opportunities to lead (and to fail), feedback, and continual "sharpening" and shaping. It is more than head knowledge; it must include hands-on exposure.

Our failure to personally oversee this process of leadership development and mentoring has produced a generation of frustrated pastors and leaders. Many leaders are frustrated because they have been thrust into positions of leadership, wanting to do their best but feeling totally inadequate for the challenge. These leaders know God has called them and that God is with them—but no one has actually shown them *how* to do what is expected of them.

So where do most leaders turn for help? Today, people looking for help will either run to the bookstore to look for a book, or if they are Internet-savvy, they will search online for help. However, there is a lack of real-life mentors in their lives. They lack someone who can guide them and advise them. Leaders need someone who can help them sort through all the information they have accumulated because they do not know how to discern the good from the "not-so-good." How do they apply what they have learned?

This is when the blame game often begins. "Why didn't we have this subject in Bible School? Why didn't someone warn me there would be days like this? No one taught me how to handle people like these." Needless to say, the list goes on. Suddenly a leader finds expectations put upon them, which they do not have the experience to handle. They feel they have been thrown into the deep end, and there is no one to toss them a life buoy.

What is needed? They need a mentor in their life to help them, just as the apostle Paul helped and mentored Timothy.

The Call for Mentors

Remember when the apostle Paul rejected a young man named John Mark because of a perceived failure during Mark's first venture into ministry? During that first opportunity to receive exposure and ministry experience with the great apostle Paul, Mark blew it.

> *These leaders know that God has called them and that God is with them—but no one has actually shown them how to do what is expected of them.*

As you know, when the time came for a second ministry trip, Paul said, "No way, he is not coming." This resulted in Paul and his ministry partner, Barnabas, separating and going in different directions in the way they would do ministry (Acts 15:37–39).

At this point, Barnabas seemed to have begun to focus on mentoring. We do not hear of him pioneering a church or establishing a great schooling institution. However, we do later see the fruits of apostle Barnabas's ministry. In 2 Timothy 4:11, we see the apostle Paul requesting for John Mark to join his team. He said it this way, "Get Mark and bring him with you, because he is *helpful to me* in my ministry."

In other words, Paul saw the good results of mentoring and now wanted the benefit of a "reject," whose destiny and calling had been redeemed because someone cared enough to mentor their God-given potential.

Later we see a "converted" apostle Paul himself beginning to mentor younger ministers. You can read all about Paul's relationship with young Timothy. We also see Paul instructing Timothy to do the same, "And the things you have heard me say in the presence of many witnesses entrust to reliable men who will be qualified to teach others" (2 Tim. 2:2).

What About You?

Let me ask you something. Could God be speaking to you about moving on and moving up into a new level of ministry yourself? Do you need to change the way you are relating to your emerging leaders? Maybe God has been speaking to you about mentoring, but you are not sure how to begin nor when. I want to challenge you to an enlarged vision.

Always remember, ministry is not about "us," it is all about "them." It is about building others up and not just building our own personal ministry. There is more at stake than our personal success.

It is time to unlock your mind and spirit so you can break free from traditional thinking that limits you to a predetermined box. That old box of yesterday will never allow you to rise to new levels. If you become limited by your past successes, then the kingdom of God will also be limited.

God cannot advance His kingdom with old thinking and old methods. He is calling a new breed of leaders who will facilitate the combined discipling and mentoring required to produce His next generation of leaders. You are a part of God's plan.

> *That old box of yesterday will never allow you to rise to new levels.*

Maybe I can say it this way—follow Jesus. Do ministry like Jesus did. Lead like He led. He took twelve unlikely men and then later commissioned them to be apostles to the nations. He entrusted the advancement of His entire ministry and kingdom on earth into their hands. Were they perfect? No. But did they turn their world upside down? Yes.

It all began with Jesus. Now Jesus expects each of us to cry out, "God, let a new wave of Your Spirit and anointing now begin to flow through me. Make me a mentor after Your own heart!"

CHAPTER 6

Leadership Transition Begins
with Leadership Development

WHERE DO LEADERS COME FROM? Where can
I find them? Do you have some leaders that you
can send over to our church or business?" These questions are being asked everywhere. We have already seen
that we cannot simply pack our emerging leaders off to
get a degree and expect them to start functioning as
a leader upon their return. Neither can we get all the
leaders we need by poaching "born" leaders.

Since leadership development does not happen by
accident, we need a structure and an intentional process
in each of our organizations to *make it happen*.

Let me illustrate this process by sharing with you
Dominic's journey from first-time visitor to senior
pastor.

Dominic's Journey

Dominic came to Trinity Christian Centre for the
very first time in 1980. He remembers it vividly.

Everything about him—his long hair, his hippie
"hole-ly" jeans—made him stand out like a sore thumb
in the congregation of a few hundred people.

As he made his way down to the altar, he remembers being embraced and prayed for by a Caucasian

lady pastor—who was none other than me! He recalls, "I was quite sure that the crowd parted to make way for me because no one wanted to come near me. I was unkempt and scruffy. Yet when I made my way down to the altar, a Caucasian lady pastor hugged me, and as tears rolled down my cheeks, she prayed for me. I felt so accepted and loved by God."

He went on to say, "Now, if you have ever been hugged by Pastor Dowdy, you know that her fragrance leaves its imprint on you. The scent was on me all day! I was filled with the Holy Spirit that day."

Dominic had many starts and stops in his walk with God. He was in and out of church in those early days of his Christian walk. I must say that the tenacity of our spiritual parents in Carecells was a "God-given strategy" that worked in his life. I think I can say he was worse than John Mark! He would come into church and then disappear again. This cycle happened over and over.

Finally, because I saw a God-given potential in him, I prayed and asked God for divine help. "God, help us keep the 'hook' set in him long enough for Your divine call and purpose to be developed in his life." One of our spiritual parents kept after him, calling him, and checking on him until God completed the work for that stage of his life. Dominic describes it this way:

> "The spiritual parents were people who had a tenacious belief in people, because they believed that God was a God of the second chance. This was a value Pastor Dowdy had instilled in the church."

Dominic himself became a spiritual parent, sharing his faith and nurturing new believers, and then a Carecell leader, leading a small group of believers that grew and eventually multiplied. He later grew into the role of a sectional leader, with an increased sphere of responsibility over a cluster of Carecells in the central part of Singapore. In that role, he mentored leaders and spiritual parents to reach out to new people and to integrate them into the church.

Carecells Develop Leaders

Let me pause for a moment to explain more about *Carecells*, so you can appreciate that it is really an ecosystem for intentional, homegrown leadership development. When I first began our small groups in Trinity Christian Centre, there were no models. I called these small groups Carecells. Today there are many different models being used by different churches, but which one should you choose?

Before you begin, first stop and ask yourself:

- What is my vision?
- What do I believe is the mandate that Jesus gave us before He left this earth?

When you have answers to these two questions, you will have some basis or guidelines to help you choose which model to use for your small groups. All the models have some good components within them, but which one will contribute to your vision and the fulfilling of God's mandate?

> *The spiritual parents were people who had a tenacious belief in people, because they believed that God was a God of the second chance.*

Carecells are not meant to be "holy huddles," where Christians just get together for fellowship. Sure, fellowship takes place as well, but there is a higher goal in each gathering. The overall goal of Carecells is to create an internal process within the church where a person can discover Christ and grow into a kingdom-minded leader who can in turn reproduce other kingdom-minded leaders.

The foundation of the Carecell model is a process I call *spiritual parenting*, through which people first experience a mentor, and then later become a mentor to someone else. A typical scenario goes like this: A pre-believer is prayed for and cared for by a spiritual parent until he makes a decision for Christ. The new believer is nurtured until he grows and becomes a spiritual parent himself. As a spiritual parent, he is equipped to reach out to pre-believers, and is mentored through his participation in the core group—comprising a leader, an associate leader, and usually at least two spiritual parents—where he learns to nurture others and picks up group leadership skills.

Instead of having people make a big leap from being a member to functioning as a leader, Carecells enable individuals to grow in their capacity and sphere of influence, to be proven at one level (that of a spiritual parent), before being tested for faithfulness at the next level (that of an associate leader and then a leader).

Creating Strategic Leadership Opportunities

The goal of every Carecell is to multiply itself. This, I am convinced, is necessary for meaningful relationships and effective leadership development to take place. When the group has grown too large to be cared for adequately by the existing leader

The Carecell is really an ecosystem for intentional, homegrown leadership development.

and core group, the Carecell multiplies into two. This is usually a celebratory occasion, as it means that more lives have been reached and more people have become connected to the family of God. It means the Carecell has fulfilled its very purpose of existence.

Get this: the multiplication of a Carecell strategically creates an opportunity for an associate leader to step up to the plate to be the leader of the new group. A new leader is born, new spiritual parents are commissioned, and new people serve as hosts and open their homes for the weekly Carecell meeting—*everyone* moves on and moves up in God.

Carecell leaders are conscious of the need for leadership renewal or succession planning at a micro level. Here's why: They know that their goal is to multiply their *cell*, but they know they can't do that unless they also multiply them*selves*. Hence, it has become second nature for them to identify potential leaders and to partner with their sectional leaders and pastors to mentor these emerging leaders. You could say that Care-cells instill into the very fabric of a church, the *culture* of helping others move on and move up in God.

❂ Having functioned within a core group from the very start of their leadership journey, it becomes easy for these leaders to begin to function in team ministry. It is a model of shared responsibility. So from the beginning, they learn to function in team ministry and mutual submission. ❂

In the Carecell structure, a sectional leader oversees a cluster of Carecells. Those who do well as sectional leaders, and who sense a call of God on their lives, are then selected to be ministry interns.

However, not all ministry interns end up serving in a "full-time" capacity. Some become lay pastors, excelling both in the church and in the marketplace. Nonetheless, this creates a definitive pool from which key leaders emerge. Today, Trinity has a pool of 100 sectional leaders, and new leaders are added to our leadership base every quarter.

Create an internal process within the church where a person can discover Christ and grow into a kingdom-minded leader who can in turn reproduce other kingdom-minded leaders.

If you want to know more, you can visit my website www.naomidowdy.com or Trinity's website www.trinity.net. At either of these places, you will find information about how to contact us for more details about the Carecell model for your church.

A Leader in the Making

Follow with me as we continue on Dominic's journey as an emerging leader in Trinity Christian Centre. By this time, the unstable convert had blossomed into a leader. Throughout this time, he was taking classes in our Lay Leadership Institute, which had been set in place to provide formal training for our growing numbers of lay leaders. He later went to Bible school, and one of our pastors continued part of the mentoring until I began to take an active role in his development for the future.

Carecells instill into the very fabric of a church the culture of helping others move on and move up in God.

As part of his development, Dominic was assigned a major outreach project—the Singing Christmas Tree on Orchard Road, Singapore's prime shopping district—as well as numerous other projects in the church, including evangelistic dramas like *The Master's Plan*. All these took place even before he came in as a staff member.

I considered these to be training and mentoring opportunities for emerging leaders—not just Dominic. I rotated among different leaders the responsibility of overseeing these major projects. The purpose was to observe. How would they lead? How would people respond to their leadership? How well would they resolve challenges that would arise? Thus, these assignments were for the purpose of developing their leading, planning, organizing and strategizing skills.

It also exposed them to multi-functional leadership.

In case you lose a staff member for some reason, at least there would be others who know something about each area of ministry and have had a measure of exposure in overseeing it.

Dominic was one of the many lay leaders we had in Trinity, but his calling became evident as he served in each of these roles, each one larger than the one before. By the time he came in full-time, he was already a serious candidate for a major leadership role in the church.

Your church structure is probably different, but the issue is the same. Do you have a structure that facilitates the involvement of lay people in leadership roles? I don't mean the faithful ones who are always doing 80 percent of the work, but a "revolving" structure that is always assimilating new people and getting them involved in kingdom work and doing so at increasing levels of influence and leadership.

They should be doing more than just having the title of "leader." They should be leading, praying, speaking into people's lives, and inspiring others. In other words, they should *be* a leader—not just a manager carrying out instructions.

Delegate Your Authority

If you want to develop leaders—not just managers—you must model respect for delegated authority and practice mutual submission. I was intentional in creating this culture within Trinity Christian Centre. Pastor Dominic describes it this way:

"**Trinity was never run as a personality-driven church**. Pastor Dowdy was careful to ensure that mutual submission and true team ministry was the order of the day. This is the essential DNA that has been established in Trinity Christian Centre."

What is mutual submission? Mutual submission is respect for delegated authority, *even if* you are the most senior leader in the organization. Let me describe it this way: you cannot simply delegate responsibilities; you must also delegate the authority needed to get the job done.

For example, although I was the senior pastor, if anyone came to me with concerns about, say, the creative ministry, I would listen to their concerns but always point them back to our creative ministry pastor. I had delegated my authority in that area; hence, *I myself* needed to respect the chain of command I had set up. To do otherwise would be to communicate that, no matter who was put in charge, all people needed to do was to come and talk to me. This would nullify the authority of those whom I had set in place and short-circuit the mentoring process for these leaders.

> *They should be a leader—not just a manager carrying out instructions.*

This principle created the environment and the seedbed for leadership development and mentoring, because the leaders I put in place over any area knew that it was really their "baby." I was not going to step in and meddle with it, nor rescue them from their mistakes. I did, however, set goals and expectations for them. I let them come up with ideas, propose these ideas and—if these ideas were properly talked through and approved—they would test and implement them. If they had concerns or doubts, we would talk these over. But they had full ownership over their area of responsibility at all times.

I believe that this process is best for the organization because it creates a broad base of leadership instead of a narrow one, where ownership and power are concentrated on one or a few key people. More importantly, in terms of leadership development, it allows new leaders to emerge.

What Then Do *I* Do?

You may ask, "What then do *I* do?" Delegating your responsibilities does not mean you have nothing to do. Far from it! You are still overall "in charge." You do not abdicate your position. You are allowing a platform for development, along with an understanding of mutual submission. You are responsible for the development of all these leaders—to mentor them in their character and skills and to look out for new areas to which they need to be exposed.

This is far more strategic and important than doing it all by yourself. Yes, I know you can do a better job than they can, but that is not the point. The purpose is to identify emerging leaders, develop them, and groom some to the point where they can actually take over what you do. Remember, you can't move on and move up unless there is someone to whom you can hand this over.

Believe me, this is actually far more difficult than doing it all yourself. You will need great willpower to resist the overwhelming temptation of stepping in and doing it for them. This will require you to operate with a totally different mindset, but it is the only way to develop leaders. Remember, you cannot simply pack them off to Bible school or to a leadership conference; your organization is the best seedbed for the mentoring of these emerging leaders.

> *This will require you to operate with a totally different mindset, but it is the only way to develop leaders.*

Room to Grow

As you can see, leadership development is more than giving a willing worker a title. You must incorporate into your structure a complete process for the discovery of spiritual gifts and the development of those gifts and anointings. Each leader must be given delegated authority and ownership over his sphere and room to spread his wings and grow. How else will they learn to soar?

Dominic and all of our leaders are a product of this culture. It is this whole process that has enabled Trinity to produce so many strong leaders. Regardless of where they function, in the church or in the marketplace, they are strong and powerful as they walk and live a kingdom lifestyle.

Dominic says:

> "Mutual submission and team ministry create the best seedbed for leadership development and transition. This created an atmosphere that facilitated a successful handover."

We will look at team ministry in a later chapter. At this point, I want to challenge you to look beyond what you are doing now and ask, "God, what needs to change in order for me to move on and move up into my destiny? Help me change so I can develop *leaders*."

You must begin sometime, and that time needs to be *now*.

CHAPTER 7

Identifying Potential Successors

TO IDENTIFY A POTENTIAL SUCCESSOR, or to shortlist a pool of potential successors, you must first understand the kind of organization you are leading.

What kind of organization are you? Your shortlist of successors depends greatly on the kind and size of the organization you are leading.

In my case, Trinity Christian Centre had evolved far beyond the small group of forty-two believers that I inherited. It was no longer a simple local church.

Here's why.

- **Ownership of Property**—When I took over the church in 1975, it had no premise or building of its own. When I handed the church over in 2005, we had three freehold properties, and we had just started building the largest Christian complex in the nation (which is now complete).

- **Stewardship of Missions Funds**—One of the first things I did in Trinity was to hold a missions convention. Remember, they were worried about their finances and, as a result, were retreating in their faith and vision. I was convinced that if we put

God's global agenda first, He would take care of our needs as a church.

That first missions convention in 1976 saw a grand total of $35,300 in faith promises for missions. In 2005, when I handed it over, the church had close to $4.5 million in faith promises for missions. Needless to say, my successor needed to be someone who had the integrity, vision, and foresight to steward the large amount of funds for kingdom purposes.

- **Missions Impact**—Because of my apostolic calling, I was always traveling internationally to train pastors and leaders. We also had an annual international conference, where many pastors and leaders came to be trained. From a church with no missions program whatsoever, Trinity had evolved into a church of global impact, sending out missions impact teams, as well as training and consultation teams.

  When I handed it over in 2005, the church was involved in more than twenty different countries, and with more than one thousand churches and pastors, helping them take their churches and ministries to the next level. My successor needed to be someone who could relate to these organizational leaders from various cultures and earn their respect.

- **Social Impact**—Because of my call to impact the community and the nation in practical ways, I had founded a social arm that ministers to the poor, families of prison inmates, the elderly, and disadvantaged children from low-income or dysfunctional families, who were having learning difficulties in school.

> *My successor needed to be someone who had the integrity, vision, and foresight to steward a large amount of funds for kingdom purposes.*

- **Training College**—With my call to train leaders, I had established TCA College, which started as a training institute for our lay leaders, and later became a Bible college, offering full-fledged degree programs at both bachelor's- and master's-degree levels.

Whoever took over the church would also have to lead these other entities. It was a multiple portfolio, a complex creature. In business terms, the church was more akin to a multi-national corporation than a typical local church.

> *Whoever took over the church would also have to lead these other entities. It was a multiple portfolio, a complex creature.*

Understand why I am sharing this about Trinity. I only share these things to illustrate that (knowing the kind of church we had become) it became evident to me that Trinity Christian Centre needed a leader who walked and functioned with the mantle of an apostle and prophet. This leader must know how to assemble the right team with the variety of anointings needed for the diverse arenas in which God has called the church to flow and function.

It became obvious that we could not have a leader who was mostly pastoral, nor could we have a leader who was mostly teacher-gifted. We could not have a leader who was mostly an evangelist—and yet, all these gifts are important and must be present within the church. Yes, we need pastors, teachers, and evangelists, and their accompanying anointing. However, without the right leader, these other gifts would not be able to be released to function in the church as they should.

Hence, you must look for the spiritual gift(s) needed to lead your church or business. You should be able to identify the various gifts God has placed within your organization. It is your responsibility as a leader to then ask yourself: where in the church/business structure does each spiritual gift fit best—in order for everyone to fulfill their destiny and calling in God?

Before You Choose

Some early factors to consider would be:

- Size of the organization
- Size of the staff
- Vision of the organization
- Values of the organization
- What kind of church/organization are you? Who is your target community? Are you located in the

countryside, in a college town, a retirement area, or in a busy urban center?

- Does the church/organization have multi-level ministries or departments?
- Have you raised spiritual sons or daughters—leaders from within the organization?
- What spiritual gift(s) are needed to take the church/organization into its destiny?
- Always remember that leadership involves influence. Will your successor be able to influence the same sphere of people you presently influence and even beyond your present sphere?

Once you have properly identified the kind of organization you are, you can begin to identify the kind of leaders you will need. You will need to find the right match.

Key Areas of Consideration

After taking into consideration the kind of organization you are leading, and the giftings present in your team, you should begin to look at the personal qualities of your team to see who might be among your potential successors.

We live in a time of fast-changing social landscapes and economic conditions, with an increase in natural disasters—all of these will cause fear to rise up in people's hearts. Thus, you must choose a strong leader who can build faith and confidence in people, so they will trust God through these turbulent times.

Character

Throughout the world today, everyone—from governments to financial institutions and churches—is crying out for leaders of character, for men and women they can trust. Leaders that are motivated by a personal agenda of greed or power cannot solve the circumstances and crises that are shaking our world today.

You must choose a strong leader who can build faith and confidence in people, so they will trust God through these turbulent times.

Therefore, in your selection process, one of the key considerations should be the person's **character**. If they seem to possess spiritual gifts or anointing, but not godly character, it is not acceptable. There are many reasons for this, which are too numerous to elaborate on in this book.

Suffice to say, that when you see major character flaws in someone who has a lot of potential, you cannot assume that the person will change after you have promoted them and put them into a higher office. Promotion does not make anyone faithful, nor does it change his or her heart. There must be consistent faithfulness and loyalty *first*.

If you are never sure where the person is in their dealings with those around them, then you are in trouble. If you are always questioning their motives and sincerity, take these as a warning from God. This is not going in the right direction.

If you see them more focused on themselves and

their importance, and grappling for power, again stop and look *beyond* potential. God gives potential to all of us. Sad to say, many with great potential never achieve that potential because they do not deal with character issues early in their life.

> *You need to check their heart, because you cannot teach "heart."*

You and the organization must be able to operate and function with full trust in the person. God has the right person, in the right place, for the right time, with the right motives, and the right gifts for the assignment. You need to check their heart, because you cannot teach "heart." Their heart relates to character.

Capacity

Whoever is your choice must also have the grace to step into the new level of leadership before them. In other words, they must possess the capacity and the needed ability to get the job done. The overall capacity of the person must be taken into consideration. It is not about being a good Christian or even a prayerful person. Everyone has a certain God-given capacity. Be careful not to promote someone to a level of incompetence.

Remember how Jethro instructed Moses to put some over thousands, hundreds, fifties, tens, and so forth? Jethro was wisely telling Moses to be aware of the different capacities that people have at a given time and season. We must not promote people into a new level of leadership that is beyond their capacity to achieve.

Sure, new levels will definitely challenge and stretch your successor. However, it should not be so far beyond their God-given capacity that they just cannot achieve it. Again this is a very delicate area to assess.

I do believe that a person can grow and develop, thus increasing their capacity; then a door of greater opportunity can be available to them. We need to be discerning as to where a person is at this time, as well as the next level they can attain as God stretches them. However, do not put them into a position where you know they will probably fail. How soon can we release them? I like to express it this way: *"As soon as possible but not prematurely."*

We need to be discerning as to where a person is at this time, as well as the next level they can attain as God stretches them.

On the threshold of leadership transition at a national level, Moses told the people, "The LORD your God will drive out those nations before you, little by little. You will not be allowed to eliminate them all at once, or the wild animals will multiply around you" (Deut. 7:22).

The principle here is that we cannot change and enlarge our capacity too quickly. It is a process. This underscores the need for patience and yet it is not an excuse for delay. As we grow, our capacity and ability will increase, and God will continue to enlarge our boundaries and territories—in accordance with our increased capacity for an increased sphere of authority and responsibility.

Chemistry

Another essential component is chemistry. You must like working with these people. You must like being around them. There must be a strong relationship where you are able to get along. You share the same vision and enjoy working together. There is a certain chemistry or synergy that takes place in the team when the leader is with them.

The person of choice must be able to attract other leaders to join their team. This is chemistry. It works like this. We all know it is not possible for everyone to like us. Yet even if I do not like everything about you on a personal level—I trust you. Beyond the "surface" feelings, I respect your call, I believe in your vision and God's anointing upon your life.

For that reason, when we are working together, there is a certain chemistry that takes place that enables everyone on the team to feel inspired and energized to take new territory for God. This kind of chemistry among the leadership team is essential.

By now you can begin to see how the testing and evaluation of each individual's character, capacity, and chemistry would not be possible, unless you first entrust to them some responsibilities *and* the accompanying authority. Only when you delegate authority can you begin to see what people can do with the authority you give to them.

Charisma vs. Leadership

When it comes to choosing your successor, avoid the tendency to confuse charisma with leadership. For example, we may see and hear people who are great speakers, and we can become mesmerized by them. You must realize that charisma does not necessarily make someone a good pastor or leader.

Only when you delegate authority can you begin to see what people do with the authority you give to them.

One area to watch out for, if you are leading a church, is using preaching skills as the main criteria for selecting your successor. Yes, he or she should be a good preacher, a good communicator, but that should not be the main criterion.

Neither can we use mere human wisdom to try and determine the selection of new leadership. You cannot use seniority as the measuring rod. Those are all a product of the past procedures often referred to as "old wineskin" thinking.

My Natural Family or Someone Else?

Some of you may wish to hand over your leadership position to your natural sons and daughters, but please understand that it may not be the right choice for the organization. It is wonderful if it happens, but you cannot assume that will be the case.

There will be the natural pull of your heart to want

to pass the organization on to your natural sons or daughters. You want to provide for them. But look out! Do they have the right gifts, skills, and anointing? Has God called them for this level of ministry—and are they ready at *this* time?

Do not try to create a dynasty. Here is where you must be very sensitive to God's leading and not be driven by your natural human desire. God's leader will have God's confirmed anointing and grace to handle the growing responsibilities of leadership.

Get this: there must be a calling from God and an anointing of His Spirit that releases God's grace for His assignment. God *graces* His chosen one for the level of function to which He calls him or her.

> *There must be a calling from God and an anointing of His Spirit that releases God's grace for His assignment.*

Without His grace for the leadership role, the position will break a person because he will not be able to measure up to its tasks and demands.

This underscores the importance of having a process in place to help you identify your potential successor. That process must be guided and bathed in much prayer, for God's plans for the organization—and the ability for each one to move on and move up—hang in the balance.

CHAPTER 8

Coaching Your Leadership Team

WHEN DOMINIC WAS IN BIBLE school, he was seconded to help develop the youth ministry of a pioneer church-planting effort in Singapore. After his assignment ended, he returned to serve in Trinity. He began as our youth pastor. As the church grew and we restructured, he was assigned to oversee all of the children, youth, and campus ministries, working with and giving oversight to the pastors and leaders assigned in each of these areas.

Later, he was assigned to help pioneer an outreach church in Perth, Australia. He then was assigned to pastor another outreach church in Vancouver, Canada. During those years, he also traveled with me overseas to minister in churches. He worked with me in training and consultation to establish and develop churches in our Carecell model.

If you are following closely, you will see that each assignment was training and developing him in different areas of responsibility in ministry.

All of this was very intentional. He was being mentored through different situations, and he grew in wisdom and stature.

This was not unique to Dominic. At that time, I was working simultaneously with several emerging pastors and leaders. I needed to help each of them discover their spiritual gifts and develop in those areas. This meant giving each of them different platforms where they could grow and expand in the use of their passion and gifts. It was also a platform for me to become aware of areas of weakness that would need to be improved or changed before they could move on and move up in their calling and destiny.

Structuring for Succession

In the mid 1990s, I took the church through a period of restructuring. Listen friends, sometimes our old structures will not facilitate God's new season. God's new direction and season will demand we restructure in order to accommodate and achieve God's new purposes. Do not be afraid of change—if it is under God's direction.

During this restructuring, I set in place another platform for the final development of anyone who would become my successor. I did not tell them that finding a successor was part of the objective; they only knew it was part of their leadership growth and development in ministry.

I handpicked a six-member leadership team as part of my succession plan. What this meant was that I had a plan, a process, and a platform where I could develop and test these potential successors. Dominic was one of these six, and he was growing and becoming a "son of the house."

As I worked with all six members of the leadership team, I was keenly aware that I was mentoring a team of potential successors. I felt the weight of responsibility in assessing everyone. I wanted to be sure before God that I did not play favorites, so I gave each of them equal opportunity to make their calling and election sure.

I needed to test them in other areas as well. They needed to be tested in many areas, including their character, prayer life, relationships with other leaders, views and practices concerning money, family life, values, and concept of power. They also needed to be able to communicate and train others in our Carecell model. Suffice to say, there was a lot to work on during those years.

Team Ministry

I also needed to enlarge my team's vision of how they should function and how they should see the church from an overall holistic perspective, rather than just being concerned for their own personal departments and scope of responsibility. In other words, I needed them to function in true team ministry.

I had a plan, a process, and a platform where I could develop and test these potential successors.

Functioning in team ministry goes beyond operating as a multiple-staff church. Let me explain: the old models of ministry went through several evolutions. It began with one church, one pastor. Then we evolved to one church, one senior pastor, and one youth pastor or assistant pastor. The next step was to have multiple pastors: youth, children, music, assistant pastors, etc. As many churches began to have a multiple-staff model, they thought that having multiple staff members was equivalent to team ministry.

At first glance, this might seem to be true; however, functionally it is not true. Let me highlight some problems with this model, and you can check if this has been your experience as well.

In reality, here is what happens: each staff member was hired for a specific portfolio. Thus their goal is to grow and

Functioning in team ministry goes beyond operating as a multiple-staff church.

make their specific area of ministry the best in the church. After all, that is what they were hired to do.

This sets the stage for a competition among the multiple staff members for talent from the same resource pool—the congregation. Each staff wants to recruit the best leaders and volunteers for their ministry. There is no real consideration given to what the person's gifts might actually be, and in which ministry they might function best. The goal was to attract and retain the best in their particular ministry.

Contrast this with true *team ministry*. First of all, the leadership team should be a team that represents the different gifts of the five-fold ministry. Secondly, they think, pray, and plan together for the overall church—not just for their specific department. They will even identify people who are currently serving in their specific ministry area but whose spiritual gifts indicate that they would be more effective serving in a different ministry. In meetings, these leadership team members may say, "Hey, I have this person serving in my ministry/department, whom, I think should be transferred into your ministry."

While their individual ministries are important to them, their highest concern is the development of people, so that each person can reach their highest potential in God. It is not about becoming the best or biggest department. But rather, how God can use all gifts, so His church can be the greatest and fulfill its destiny.

This principle also applies if you are leading a business or marketplace organization. Your successor needs to make that shift in his thinking, from a narrow perspective that is limited to one or two specific areas, to seeing a wider view of how the entire organization can move forward.

Don't Put All Your Eggs in One Basket

It is important to have a pool of potential successors. In fact, it is dangerous to have only one person in your succession plan, as the process is long and much can happen over a period of years.

Although Dominic was not aware, it was evident to me several years prior to the actual transition that he was going to be my successor. But there were some areas he needed to overcome, and I was waiting to see him grow in those areas. Thus I did not make the fact known to him.

Personally I do not believe in telling people in

advance, "If you keep up the good work, one day, this will all be yours." I do not believe in making such promises in advance and thus building up the hopes of a person, when there is still uncertainty or things that must take place before an announcement can be made.

The reason is simple. During the developmental years, many things can happen. There are many choices that a person must make in the course of their life and ministry. Too many things could go wrong. Also, I feel that telling people in advance can cause them to assume that the promotion is a done deal, such that they feel there is no need to pray and press into God for His enablement.

There were, in fact, a few critical junctures when I felt the succession plan was at risk. One of those times occurred when Pastor Dominic came to me

It is dangerous to have only one person in your succession plan, as the process is long and much can happen over a period of years.

sharing a possible plan for him and his wife to move to the United States. Her company at that time had an office in the U.S. and could transfer her there for work. He talked about how he could be based there for ministry and travel to South America for missions work. This location would position him to minister and work in several areas we were focusing on at that time. The plan sounded so logical. In fact, he had already talked to his wife about it, and she was in agreement to make this transition.

This presented a real challenge for me. I knew why

he should not go. Now was the time for him to stay in the home church. He had been sent overseas at other times, but now was not the time. I still did not want to let him know that he would be my successor, because there were several things in him I was still working on at that time.

This is where lots of prayer and lots of talking—without letting him know my real reasons—became critical. God answered my prayers and soon the plan was aborted. He chose to stay back and continued serving and leading in Trinity.

You may have some encounters like this. I stress again that prayer and dialogue are the only ways to deal with each challenge you will face.

Start Early

This underscores the importance of having a pool of potential successors, from whom you can eventually choose your successor. Some leaders buy into the myth that "having a pool of potential successors is a luxury that only large organizations can afford." However, this is a necessity, not a luxury.

Remember, I did not start succession planning when the church was a few-thousand strong; I started when we were only a small church of forty-two members and seventy-five problems. Yet, because there was intentional and homegrown leadership development—through spiritual parenting and Carecells—to bring individuals from the point of decision to nurturing and on to discipleship, our leadership base grew.

Without this leadership base fuelling and supporting its growth, Trinity would not have grown to where it is today.

What If I Am Not the Leader?

You may be reading this and thinking, "But I am not the senior pastor or CEO; I am just one of the leaders in my organization. How do these principles apply to me?" Listen, whoever you are and whatever you do, leadership renewal should be happening at every level of the organization.

Remember, we talked about *intentional* and *homegrown* leadership development, and how Carecell leaders are always on the lookout to identify and mentor potential leaders. So while you may not be in the position to decide who your successor might be, you should always be intentionally multiplying yourself.

If You Cannot Choose

Let me stop here for a moment. I know that while many of you are leading independent churches, some of you are part of a denomination and you are thinking, "But I cannot choose my successor. The board must choose and then the congregation must vote." With these words, you are eliminating yourself from this whole journey of succession. May I quickly say to you: wrong thinking!

Hold on and follow me please. As I have mentioned earlier, I do understand the institutional processes.

However, instead of just "dumping" the decisions on the

Leadership renewal should be happening at every level of the organization.

board or a search committee, why don't you groom and mentor some potential successors as I have mentioned? You know the persons, and you should know the church and what kind of gifts and anointing are needed to move the church to another level. Since you are the best person to know these things, you should be the person to present the name of your possible successor for them to consider.

To me, if you have done a good job, you should be able to share and convince them why your choice is the one they should consider. Your choice should also have borne fruit to validate what you are suggesting. Thus I strongly believe, regardless of the kind of church or organization you are in now, you can still have a voice in the issue of who your successor might be.

Who Is God's Choice?

It was exciting to see each of my potential successors grow in their leadership. They were all good. They all had a heart for God. Each of them was faithfully committed to each assignment given to them.

Still, there was always the nagging question: which one has the spiritual gifts and capacity to take the church forward? All of them could preach, prophesy, and lead ministries but...who was God's choice?

This required me to look beyond personal relationships, longevity in the church, their outward personalities, and their charisma in the pulpit. In the midst of the many, there was the challenge of knowing God's choice of the one who would take the church forward. ●

CHAPTER 9

Choices Determine Destiny

THERE WAS ONE AREA I saw in one of our pastors that was a disturbing trend. It was his weakness in follow-through and the necessary administration required to complete a job assignment or project well.

I would call him into my office and speak to him about this over and over. I was trying to impress upon him the urgency to improve in this area. Finally, one day I called him in and laid out a large sheet of paper before him. Putting a small box in one corner of the paper, I explained that he had a ministry and God was using him, but he was limiting himself to the small box instead of realizing his full potential, represented by the large sheet of paper.

After spending extended time going over all of this with him, I said, "I am not going to speak to you again about the need for you to have a working knowledge of administration. Everyone, regardless of what his or her spiritual gifts are, must have some working knowledge of administration. Today the choice is yours. I am not going to speak to you again on this area. If you want to reach your potential in God as a leader, you must know how to oversee and complete all assignments fully. You will need to personally seek help from Pastor Beatrice Kang (Beatrice was a staff member who had both the experience and the spiritual gift of administration). I am not going to do this for you. <u>I will know your deci-</u> <u>sion by the results I see in your performance</u>. When you walk out of this door, your future is in your hands." I prayed with him, and he left my office.

That person was Dominic, and the results of that meeting should be obvious today. <u>He sought to learn</u> <u>and develop an area of weakness.</u> *<u>His choice determined</u>* *<u>his destiny.</u>*

I Can Change, I Must Change, I Will Change!

This is the mantra I drum into everyone who attends my leadership training. Why is this important? When you coach your leadership team and develop them in their calling and destiny, you are responsible for high-lighting critical areas that can hinder or rob them of their God-given potential. <u>However, if they refuse to</u> <u>take steps to change, then it is a waste of your time and</u> <u>theirs to continue investing in them. This is hard, but</u> <u>it is reality. You cannot help someone who refuses to</u> <u>change.</u>

When I talked to some pastors to point out areas that needed to be worked on and changed in their life and ministry, they would tell me, "But I like to do things this way. I cannot change." <u>When someone you</u> <u>are mentoring says they cannot change, or worse, that</u> <u>they will not change—look out! That is a warning sign</u> <u>to you.</u>

They are saying, "I am set in my ways and refuse to grow." To me, this is serious and can eliminate someone from consideration. Why? They are not demonstrating a learning posture. We must always be open to learn and

When someone you are mentoring says they cannot change, or worse, that they will not change—look out!

grow, no matter how young or how old we may be.

My talk with Dominic took place many years ago. If he had not made a choice to change and develop in an area most of us really don't feel "called to" (yes, there are exceptions), he would never have been able to shoulder the responsibilities he carries today as senior pastor of Trinity Christian Centre.

Discerning God's Choice

While all of the potential successors had outstanding qualities, I made my choice through much prayer and the leading of the Holy Spirit. Since my choice would impact many people, and knowing the delicate situations that I needed to navigate, I felt there was no one I could share my plans and thinking with at that time. I could not risk the person of choice hearing about my thinking. This was an intense time of prayer for me, and it should be for you as well.

I cannot overstate the need and importance of prayer in this process. You must pray and hear what the Holy Spirit is saying until you can confidently declare: "We prayed—and it seemed good to the Holy Spirit to set aside   **ʙᴏʏ**   for the work to which God has called him/her."

Each of you must come to that place of knowing

whom God has chosen—and not who might be the most natural choice. It is an awesome responsibility, and you cannot afford to make a mistake. The destiny of the Church of Jesus Christ and His people are at stake.

Things That Were Crucial

Remember the things that I mentioned about the size and the kind of organization we were? With all of those taken into consideration, and considering all the giftings present in Trinity at that time, here were my reasons for choosing Dominic:

Dominic is a man of vision; he hears from God. I saw him as a prophet to the nations and a personal prophet to me. I also saw him as an emerging apostle. The mantle of an apostle was already evident in his life.

He was a team player, and yet he could make the tough calls. He was not only a team player; he was a team *builder*. He had a heart to develop and mentor leaders. He wanted to see new leaders emerge, and he gave himself to helping them grow in God.

He was generous in his personal financial giving. He was a faith giver to the kingdom and to Trinity.

He was open and teachable to the Holy Spirit. He received godly counsel from others around him—and yet, he was his own man.

He knew how to take responsibility. He walks in faith and knows how to trust God, even in the areas of finances and miracles.

He displayed consistent Christian character. In times of testing, I had seen him display this consistent Christian character, which is so essential. He can be generous and compassionate, but he can also deal with the "hard" things without running away or avoiding the problem, even if it involves a friend.

Another critical area was his family. I observed how he watched over his family—and worked to keep God, family, and career all in balance. Naturally, in ministry, this can often be a struggle. Yet, now more than ever, he and his lovely wife Chin Inn work at spending quality time together.

Over the years, he grew as one who can oversee the areas of administration and

> *You must come to that place of knowing whom God has chosen.*

finance—which are critical in the life of any organization—and yet he walks as a prophet. He had worked to develop in those areas that were not his gifting. He was open and flexible, without being compromising. Is he perfect? No, but was he committed to growth and improvement? Yes!

Dominic has never engaged in power play, nor has he strived for titles or positions. In fact, he had been willing to take a back seat while developing and pushing others forward. Yet, he was not afraid to step up to the plate, rise to the occasion, and take charge.

He is able to meet with and relate to leaders from different cultures and nations. He knows how to communicate and interact with those in senior positions without being intimidated or awed by them. He is respected and sought after by many churches and organizations overseas, by leaders who recognize his prophetic anointing and wisdom in the things of God. This was important for us, as Trinity is a global church.

Nobody's Perfect

You must know what you are looking for in your successor. However, you must always realize no person is perfect. Determine what from your list is negotiable and what is non-negotiable. Your list should not include small and petty things, but should address the critical components. Having these established guidelines will help you as you pray and seek God for His choice.

Not Another You

Be careful that you are not looking for someone who will just imitate exactly what you do now. You should not expect that to happen.

By this time, you should have built and structured your organization in such a way that you know it has a good foundation in the Word of God, and that foundation should remain. Those foundational principles will always be there. The vision and values will be there—assuming that you have moved with each of God's new seasons, and that the organization is not stuck with old archaic structures or mindsets from yesterday that are no longer relevant today. But how those are expressed must be updated with each changing generation.

The *expression* of the vision must always change, because your successor will be leading in a different season or era. I saw myself as a Moses. I took a people who were not a people and made them into a people of God. I established them. But now my successor must lead them and build them into a mighty army for the Lord.

You are not looking for someone who will just imitate exactly what you do now.

CHAPTER 10

Transition Is a Process
Not an Event

ONCE YOU ARE SURE OF your choice, naturally the first person to talk to is the person you have chosen. You must now talk with them so they can pray and hear from God. They must also be convinced that this is God's calling for them. You must allow them time to pray and to talk to their spouse, if they are married. It will be a joint commitment.

When the person has heard from God and can confirm that they are willing to accept the challenge of the new position, the next step is to share it with your governing board (if you have one).

This is a time of prayer and consensus building until there is full agreement among this level of leadership concerning the choice you have made. You must give them a little time to get used to the idea that you are *really* going to step aside and release this organization to a new leader. In some cases, they will prevail upon you to stay on. This is natural, as they know you and they are used to your leadership style.

You have brought them this far, and you have helped mould their life in God. At first, it is hard for them to imagine having someone else as their leader. Be careful—do not be swayed by their shortsightedness.

Do not let your ego become inflated until it causes you to lose sight of God's long-term plan and His timing.

Level-by-Level Communication Process

After the top level of governance has accepted the choice for their new senior pastor, then you will need to talk to the next level of leaders, usually your leadership team and your pastoral staff. If you have a leadership team from within your pastoral team (and I hope you do), then you should share with the leadership team first before sharing it with the entire pastoral team.

This process of communication, level-by-level, should continue until the entire staff (the immediate stakeholders) in the organization has heard about the choice from you personally. You should meet with one group of leaders at a time, sharing your heart with them about "passing the baton" and about your choice and why.

Give them a little time to get used to the idea that you are really going to step aside and release this organization to a new leader.

This will give each group an opportunity to hear directly from you. It will also give them a chance to pray for the chosen leader and release words of prophecy as the Lord moves in those meetings. This allows for a special time of bonding and affirmation that will be an encouragement to the new leader as he/she must soon begin leading a process of transition. Again, this will take a little time, but it is part of the necessary first steps in actualizing transition.

The last group to be informed is the total congregation or organization. They are not the last to hear the news because they are of lesser importance, but because they are the larger group, and without the prior affirmation from all of the other groups, you should never have reached this point in the process.

When the announcement is released to this largest level of stakeholders, it should be a time of celebration and the beginning of a new season of expectation. There should be a time for the laying on of hands and prayer, plus a new title should be given to your successor for this transition period.

I suggest they be given the title of "senior pastor designate." This makes it very clear that change is happening. It also makes it clear that time is being given to the new person and for the church or organization to get used to the idea of change. Change is being set in motion.

This period where the successor is appointed "designate" is a transitory time between the outgoing and the incoming leader. The time duration, however, was not cast in stone, and we did not publicly commit to any timeframe. In reality, I told Dominic, "I am ready when you are." I was waiting for him to *feel* ready and prepared, because the congregation was a large one, spanning many age groups.

In slightly less than two years, he felt he had everything in place, and that the team was ready for the completion of the transition.

Dominic's Perspective

Here is what Dominic said about this period of time:

"There was great wisdom in giving me time to adjust to the handover process. This was unlike many transitions of leadership I know of, where the predecessor generally hands over at an appointed time, which is usually almost immediately after the board approves the candidate.

In our context, Pastor Dowdy gave me time to settle into the idea of my new leadership position. At the same time, she was also providing a 'covering' for me during this period of adjustment, a covering both for me and for the congregation. This was important, as it allowed me the time to understand the scope of my new responsibilities and its expectations.

I strongly believe that without this protracted period of time given to me, I probably could not have handled the high expectations that came along with the position.

Neither would I have been able to discern between the right and wrong expectations. This context of new responsibilities—with the mentoring presence and covering provided by Pastor Dowdy—gave me the assurance that I was not transiting into failure but that we were transitioning from strength to strength."

Time and Space

Let's look at why the time frame that Pastor Dominic refers to as "space" is so important. Firstly, although I was not the founding pastor of Trinity Christian Centre, I was the one God brought in to *establish* the work.

There was a long journey of change and development for the church—almost thirty years. During that time, I saw most of the congregation come to Christ, receive water baptism, grow in the Lord, and become leaders in the church. Then I had the privilege of marrying them, dedicated their babies to the Lord, and counseled many of them through difficult seasons in their life. Naturally, they were attached to me.

Historically, pastors of long tenure are hard to follow, because of the many and long attachments formed over so many years. Thus extra effort and space are needed in order to allow time for emotional adjustments to be made. It is not a transfer of trust—it is really an *expansion* of trust. This is just the reality of human nature.

Yes, they should continue to honor the predecessor, but the people must also embrace a new pastor with equal loyalty and commitment. This must begin at a new level after the announcement is released. It will take time for the new leader to be fully accepted and for the reality of the weight of his/her new responsibilities to hit home and

Extra effort and "space" are needed in order to allow time for emotional adjustments to be made.

become a settled fact. This is why the role of the predecessor is so critical during this time.

Space for Enlargement of Hearts

Pastor Dominic calls this "space." He was given space and the opportunity for this enlargement in the hearts of the people to take place. He describes it this way:

> "Besides time in the handover process, space was also given for me and the congregation to adjust to each other at a new level. This was good as it allowed me, the new incoming senior pastor, space to discover and extend my leadership 'wings' at a new level.
>
> This 'space bubble' was created by Pastor Dowdy's frequent trips overseas for ministry. She would also lengthen her times away from the church. This helped to give the congregation time to experience my leadership at this new level. There was time and space for them to begin to see me with new eyes. It also provided the space for me to work with my new team and develop plans for the future. Yet, throughout this time there was also the security in the minds of the congregation that Pastor Dowdy was coming back. She had not 'deserted' nor abandoned us."

Time to Calibrate the Vision

After the announcements are all made, the steps to actualize the details need to be worked on. This internal process of planning, team building, and learning to walk with new expectations will take time.

A definite part of the transition must also include the new pastor developing his/her own team and then having time to meet, pray, and plan together for the next lap.

One day, in a meeting, a member of the new leadership team (handpicked by Dominic, not me) asked me, "Pastor, what is your vision for the next ten years?" I replied, "Wrong question. The issue is not 'What is my vision,' but 'What is *your* vision?'"

I was positive that the values, vision, and foundations laid in the church would always be there. But times and seasons change. The demographics of society change, as does the whole spiritual climate over our cities and nations. While the foundations for the organization will not change, the expression of the vision built on those foundations will need to change. For this reason, the new pastor needs to have space to meet with the new team to plan and chart the course for the coming season.

Dominic called this the time to "calibrate the vision." He expressed it this way:

> "Too often, in many transitions, the new leader simply overhauls the entire vision and replaces it with a totally new vision statement. This did not

happen with us. While Pastor Dowdy was still in office, she allowed me to put in place the new components for the expression of the vision.

This helped tremendously, in that this could all be done before the actual transition. It meant that everything would be in place for acceleration once the transition was complete. There would not be a lull or time void between leaders.

While the people understood that 'new management' would do things differently and have new expressions of the vision, there was

> *Everything would be in place for acceleration once the transition was complete.*

not a total throwing out of the old, with something new and strange being thrust upon the organization. If that were to happen, it would have caused much unnecessary unrest for the congregation.

We also did not have the problem, unlike many transitions where a lot of criticism amongst the outgoing and incoming leaders takes place. If this kind of 'infighting' and struggle were to happen, it would cause the congregation to be split in loyalties, when in fact the leadership should be standing together and pointing the congregation's loyalties towards God.

I thank God for a positive role model of mutual support and mutual submission during the time of transition. As the outgoing leader, she gave her affirmation publicly and in private to help pave the way for a successful transition."

Your Role of Support

You have read the words of Pastor Dominic and his feelings about the transition process. I hope you can hear his heart and understand how critical your role and responsibility is to the new leader during transition. He adds:

> "In most transitions, a new leader is thrust immediately into tasks, functions, and expectations without this luxury of time and space and either makes too many mistakes or makes too many changes, while trying to prove himself.
>
> In our context, space was accorded for changes to be made under the 'covering' of the outgoing leader. This allowed for affirmation from Pastor Dowdy, which strengthened me as the incoming senior pastor and it strengthened my team."

Remember, you must give the new leader your full backing and support. *What* you communicate and *how* you communicate, and the words that you choose will be subject to forensic scrutiny. Every word you say will be dissected by the people to see if there are any hidden messages in what you are saying. It is just human nature.

By conscientious identification and shared leadership events, you are to build up the new person and cause a transfer of trust from you to the new leader. The people have known you for years and they trust you; now you must encourage them to transfer and to *expand* that same trust to include the new leader. You do this by identification and by words of affirmation that you speak on many occasions.

It is through these times of association and inclusion in the different events in the life of the church that you are demonstrating your confidence and faith in the new leader. This will strengthen and hasten the acceptance of the new leader with all the stakeholders, congregation, and staff. This is an important part of ensuring a successful transition.

Shoes or Shoulders?

Pastor Dominic recalls:

> "Due to Pastor Dowdy's heart as a leader, she did not expect me to step in and fill her shoes. Instead, she encouraged and enabled me to grow and confidently walk in my own shoes and to be strong in my own identity."

Let me say here that it is old thinking that one's successor should come in and try to fill my shoes. I felt strongly that Dominic should not come in to try and fit into my shoes—he was to walk in his own shoes, but begin by standing on my shoulders!

He did not need to start from scratch; instead, he was to begin from the vantage point of all God had done through my leadership.

He was to walk in his own shoes, but begin by standing on my shoulders.

Remember, if we transition well, there is no need for a new leader to come in and "tear down" what has been built. Instead, he stands on the vantage point of your shoulders and moves on and moves up to the next level, taking the organization forward into God's new seasons.

Regardless of who you are and when you make your transition, never limit your successor to the size of your shoes. In fact you might say he/she will need to *take off* their shoes in order to stand on your shoulders.

Let's break out of old thinking and old language about shoes and the size of shoes! Rather, let's talk about calling and enablement of God for each new season.

It's time for enlargement and expansion!

CHAPTER 11

Pitfalls to Avoid

TRANSITION IS A MANY-SIDED COIN. It is not straightforward. Let me explain. What should you be doing during these final months of your ministry as pastor of the church or leader of the organization? One swing of emotion is to hurry and implement everything new you can, because this is your last chance to get some of your pet projects or programs rolling in the church.

Hold on. You must resist that temptation. You should not start anything new, you should not hire any new staff, and you should not try to cast new vision. If any of those things must be done, they must be done with the consultation and agreement of the new leaders coming in. You may be thinking, "Boy, this can be a frustrating time"—and you are right.

It may seem frustrating for a little while, but you have a higher goal in mind. Sure, in some ways things might slow down, but it is only for a short time. It should work like a relay race. All the runners are in place. One runner is off and running and doing very well, yet soon it will be time to pass the baton to a new runner.

Slow Down or Speed Up?

The runners waiting to receive the baton do not stand still and idle; they are beginning to move forward. They are starting to build up speed. Then once the baton is passed, they can accelerate and press forward with a greater sense of purpose and destiny. Leadership transition should happen the same way. There is a slowing down (not stopping, but a slowing down) of the present leader in order to allow the new leader coming in enough time to prepare the expressions of the vision after the time of handover. Working with the new leader, the outgoing leader could even begin to help pave the way for upcoming changes so that people begin to expect change and receive it in a positive manner. This is teamwork in the midst of transition.

Remember John the Baptist, speaking of Jesus and his emerging ministry, said, "He must increase, but I must decrease" (John 3:30, NAS). In essence, he was saying, "Jesus must move on and move up...I am just preparing the way."

As forerunners of our successors, you and I must have that same spirit so that we do not jeopardize the transition from one season of God-appointed leadership to another.

Pitfalls to Watch Out For

I have given you many areas to watch out for as we have discussed the journey of transition. Let me now give you a list of additional pitfalls to watch out for along the way to and after transition.

- **Don't start too late.** You must remember that transition takes time. You should begin early enough with the process so that you will not need to hurry or be pushed to take shortcuts. However, as I mentioned in an earlier chapter, if you find yourself in need of executing an accelerated transition plan, do call in someone with experience to assist and guide you through the many complex issues that you will face along the way.

- **Don't try to change everything.** At this point in the life of the church or organization, you should not try to change everything before transition. Neither should you try to execute major changes in regard to your own personal ministry too quickly. You will need a proper amount of time for prayer, communication, and preparation to take place in order to ensure that your transition will be successful.

- **Don't leave known problems or potential problem staff** for your successor to "clean up." At this moment, you have better relationships and trust (hopefully), thus it is your responsibility to clean up problematic issues, personnel, relationships, or policies while you are still the leader. Do not pass your problems on to the new person. These all developed under your leadership; thus you should resolve them. I was able to say to Pastor Dominic, "I have taken care of my giants; now you will only need to fight the new ones."

Here's an example: Personally I wanted to review the overall structure of the church to streamline all of our procedures. As any organization grows, you begin to have an "add on" in one area and then in another area, until you end up having a very cumbersome set of procedures to be followed. I felt we needed to review all of these and streamline all procedures for more efficient operations. I reckoned it would be better done on my watch, than to have the new leader come in and overhaul the entire system, and face resistance.

I initiated a whole study and review of the church, from ministry to administration, to possible needed constitutional changes, to financial procedures—and included the new pastor in the whole process. Why? This is necessary because the new leader would need to live with the consequences of all changes made during this time. Therefore, it is only proper and ethical for the new leader to be included in the whole process. They should not be merely

You should not start anything new, you should not hire any new staff, and you should not try to cast new vision.

supportive, but in genuine agreement with any changes considered.

- **Don't hire or make new appointments of people** into positions within the organization during the transition period without consulting the new incoming leader. Your successor must have the freedom to build his or her own team and not be saddled with your choices.

- **Don't make plans for the future of the organization.** It is not proper for you to create a future and expect them to fit into the "box" of your thinking.

- **Don't be suspicious** when there are meetings held without you. The new leader must be able to form his or her own leadership team and work with them in the planning and shaping of the future. Your responsibility is to give them space—for them to hear from God and prepare for the challenges they will face as the crossing over takes place. (Be careful because some of their choices or decisions may touch a sensitive nerve in your emotions; yes, you are human after all!)

- **Avoid making comments** to any stakeholders that could give them a hint that you are unhappy about decisions or the direction of things in the organization.

- **Avoid gathering people around you** who may still want to come to you for counseling or advice. You can listen to them and pray for them, but you must always direct them to their new leader.

- **Do not create a sub-group or clique** within the organization that looks to you as their immediate leader instead of the new leader. All stakeholders must receive and accept God's new appointed leader as their leader and not try to divide loyalties.

- **Do not try to compete with the new leader for attention** from the stakeholders. Swallow your pride and support the new leader. Remember they must increase and you must decrease.

- **Never take for granted** that all of your older leaders, who have been loyal to you, will be loyal to the new leader. Rule number one: never assume anything. If they cannot accept the new leader for any reason, you must resolve and clear up all of these issues before the actual transition. Their reasons may include, new leader—new vision, new leader is younger than they are, they don't like the change of leadership style, or they are comfortable with you because they feel they can control you but not the new person. Regardless of the reason, this must be resolved before the handover.

- **Do not suddenly announce a transition** without first going through the step-by-step, level-by-level process of communication that I described earlier. Communication and how you communicate are critical.

- **Do not allow organizational politics** to play a part in the process. There should be a culture in the organization where leaders acknowledge the gifts they have. Instead of jealousy or envy, there should be the acknowledgement and celebration of anointing, as was the case with Elisha.

- **Do not retain staff members who are unhappy, hurt, or unwilling** to accept the new leader.

The transition period is when you slow down, and your successor picks up speed. Soon, it will be time for the actual passing of the baton. Don't blink. This will be among your life's finest moments. Anytime a leader voluntarily steps aside to make room for his successor, the world catches a glimpse of true greatness. Be warned though—it will not be easy to let go.

CHAPTER 12

Time for Handover

Transit Well; Exit Graciously

TAKE IT FROM ME: TRANSITION is a roller-coaster ride on your emotions. I think it is a lot like a father walking his daughter down the aisle to be married to a young man. You know it is right, you know it is time, but it hurts to let her go. It is a potent mixture of sorrow and joy all scrambled up together.

Face it; your spiritual kids have grown up. You have done well. Now is the time when you must let go. Now is the time for moving on and moving up to a whole new level of significance.

It is never easy to let go. How you handle yourself through this transition will test your maturity, your ethics, your ego, your pride—it will test you in just about every area of your life.

I share this with you so you can pray and try to prepare yourself for the roller-coaster ride your emotions will experience—not just once but over and over again as different situations arise.

Now is the time for several things to take place. Your releasing, your setting in, your stepping back and then building a new relationship with everyone: board, staff, congregation.

In other words, you must develop new relationships

with all the stakeholders in the organization for the new season ahead.

Lose a Leader or Gain a Leader?

As Dominic explains:

> "In many transitions, once the handover is complete, the outgoing leader leaves town. This can further accentuate the sense of loss in the hearts and minds of all the stakeholders, especially if they are loyal to the outgoing leader and maybe still struggling with the new leader. Again this is dealing with human emotion.
>
> In our context, the affirmation, encouragement, and protracted sharing of public platforms together with Pastor Dowdy were important, as it helped assure the congregation that they were in safe hands—they did not feel abandoned; instead they felt secure both during and after the transition.
>
> This sharing of public platforms takes place when both leaders stand together before the congregation on different occasions. This visual image sends a strong message that unity, trust, respect, and honor are in place. When this message is registered in the mind and heart of the stakeholders, there is continuity in their 'follower-ship' to the new leader."

As you can see, there is a lot of human emotion that needs to be taken into account throughout the whole journey. The emotions we are dealing with are all positive emotions and natural feelings, as there is a good bond with the outgoing leader.

However, the reverse is true as well. If the relationship between the outgoing leader and the stakeholders is not strong or positive, there will be some extra emotions to be dealt with in this

> *How you handle yourself through this transition will test you in just about every area of your life.*

whole journey. I will not have time to deal with all of those in these chapters, but if you need help, just send me an e-mail.

Hands Off—Exit Graciously

Let me say this to all older leaders: learn how to let go. Learn how to not interfere or talk to congregational members in any way that would signal doubt or disapproval of the new leader. This will bring confusion, division, and undermine the new leader's authority. It is ungodly and unethical.

In the past, older leaders were expected to leave town after turning the organization over to a new leader. This was required because too often, when an older leader stayed back in the same church or same organization, they could not stay out of the operations of the organization. They functioned like a backseat driver.

This would often result in the new leader and stakeholders becoming so frustrated that the new leader would resign and leave, creating even greater problems for the overall organization and for its future growth and success.

It has been a shame that older outgoing leaders have developed this kind of a reputation. It has happened because those who have stayed on in the organization after the transition did not know how to properly release the work and stay out of the operations. Or, they still wanted too much preaching time or teaching time. Thus it became necessary to ask them to leave town. We all know you cannot have two heads. Someone has to go! This is necessary in order for the organization to be able to move forward.

When this happens, it may result in many people being hurt. Resentment can begin to develop in the hearts of people. They will not understand and will feel the new leader is not respectful and honoring of the older leader, and they will begin to harbor ill feelings toward the new leader. In reality, it was not so; it was the older leader who continually meddled in the affairs of the organization—something they should not be doing.

Always reinforce who the leadership team is and have them direct their questions to the new leader.

Same People, New Relationships

The ideal picture would be for the older leader to stay connected to the organization and still be engaged in the life of the organization. But this is possible only if the outgoing leader knows how to conduct himself and

112

relate to every level of the organization with the proper code of ethics and protocol.

That being the desired outcome, how should you relate to the stakeholders after the handover?

Reality: You are now *not* the senior leader.

Reality: People still love you and want to relate to you.

Reality: Learn how to walk in this new relationship.

Let's hear from Pastor Dominic. He knows me, he knows how I function, and most of all, he knows my heart. Here's what Pastor Dominic says:

> "Our transition was unlike other transitions I know of, where the outgoing leader continues to provide counsel to the stakeholders and this evolves into a separate sub-group within the organization.
>
> I see Pastor Dowdy in her kingdom-mindedness always pointing the congregation to me and my team whenever someone comes to her. While she may counsel them and pray with them, inevitably she points them back to the team.
>
> This is important for a couple of reasons. Firstly, if the outgoing leader stays back in the church, this constant referral to the team helps remind the stakeholders who is in the place of authority, the new senior leader, and she does not undermine the set-in leadership. Secondly, this referral is a continual affirmation of the new leadership."

This really describes how your new relationships should function. Sure, you can have friends over for dinner. You can counsel them and pray with them, but you must always reinforce who the leadership team is and have them direct their questions to the new leader, as he would be in a better position to answer their questions.

The same is true with board members or individuals at other levels of leadership within the organization.

The "No Leprosy" Policy

Remember, you do not have leprosy, and you need not shun people. However, it is imperative that you live and relate to all the stakeholders in a godly manner, guided by proper ethics and protocol. When you follow these guidelines, the transition should be successful. The people can continue to love you and relate to you. The leaders can benefit from all your years of wisdom and experience when they are confronting new challenges in the organization and in their personal lives.

Singapore as a Nation

I mentioned earlier that Singapore's former Prime Minister (now minister mentor) Lee Kuan Yew had modeled for the world an effective transition of leadership. He handed over his role as prime minister to a chosen

In the beginning, Dominic served on my team, but now I serve on his team.

leader, who was affirmed by other members of the team. This process is called leadership renewal. The veteran statesman stayed on and continues to serve as a minister mentor to avail his wisdom to the younger team. He has also used his reputation and relational capital to win friends and extend the influence of the nation.

Likewise, after the transition and until today, I am still involved in Trinity. I serve as a mentor and advisor to the new senior pastor, as well as to the board and all the stakeholders in the church. However, note the reversal of roles. In the beginning, Dominic served on my team, but now I serve on *his* team. It is still team ministry but with different roles and responsibilities.

Lee Kuan Yew developed a successful transition plan that has been followed by his successors. The nation of Singapore has grown and developed under the leadership of each new prime minister.

Likewise, in Trinity I developed a successful transition plan, and the church has grown under the leadership of the new senior pastor. I believe the same succession plan will be followed in the years to come in Trinity as well.

CHAPTER 13

Change of Command
Completing the Transition Process with a Bang

YOU HAVE IDENTIFIED WHAT KIND of church or organization you are. You have chosen your successor after a long process of leadership development that had begun much earlier. You have communicated to all the stakeholders, group by group. You have given your successor time and space to prepare his/her team. Now those preparations are complete.

Suddenly you realize there is no real model for this. In many transitions, there is not much emphasis on the actual service. The usual process is to just make a simple public announcement, lay hands on the person and pray a single prayer over him. The new leader will then release his inaugural message as the new leader to all the stakeholders. Then there is a prayer and everyone goes home.

Evangelicals and Pentecostals have an aversion towards things perceived to be from old church traditions. We do not wish to be identified with "religious" rituals, tokens, or icons. As a result, we have lost many such meaningful elements in our Christian faith. In fact, some just want to pray and get it over as soon as possible!

This attitude nullifies the importance and impact of this time in the spirit realm. Being well aware that this model of the public side of leadership transition needed review and revision, I prayed for a new way to communicate the impact of what was transpiring in the heavens during this occasion.

Setting in the New Leader

Observing from the Scriptures, the transition in leadership from Moses to Joshua was more than just a prayer. There was a release of leadership and also an impartation of anointing and authority.

We do not wish to be identified with "religious" rituals, tokens, or icons. As a result, we have lost many such meaningful elements in our Christian faith.

In Numbers 11:17, God said to Moses, "I will come down and speak with you there, and *I will take of the Spirit that is on you and put the Spirit on them*. They will help you carry the burden of the people so that you will not have to carry it alone."

Later on, in Numbers 27:15–22, we see that:

Moses said to the Lord, "May the LORD, the God of the spirits of all mankind, appoint a man over this community to go out and come in before them, *one who will lead them out and bring them in*, so the LORD's people will not be like sheep without a shepherd."

So the LORD said to Moses, "Take Joshua son of Nun, a man in whom is the spirit, and lay your hand on him. Have him stand before Eleazar the priest and the entire assembly and *commission him in their presence. Give him some of your authority*

so the whole Israelite community will obey him.
He is to stand before Eleazar the priest, who will
obtain decisions for him by inquiring of the Urim
before the LORD. ***At his command*** he and the
entire community of the Israelites will go out, and
at his command they will come in." Moses did as
the LORD commanded him...

I felt that we should be doing the same thing. We were
not installing a new pastor; we were, in reality, experi-
encing a change of command. During this service there
would be a divine shift taking place in the spirit realm:

- There was going to be a shift from my command to
  his command—with all of heaven's authority behind
  this transaction.
- I would also be releasing a new level of power and
  authority into the life of the new leader.

We called it a "Change of Command Service," and
planned it in such a way that it would be a solemn yet
inspiring event. It was to be a grand and joyous occasion
to mark a historic milestone in the life of the church.

Change of Command Service

Careful planning was done to ensure that in this
Change of Command Service, weight was given to
honor the outgoing leader with affirmation from friends
and leaders of the church. These people were on stage to
affirm and witness this event.

At the same time, these people were involved in praying, releasing prophetic words, and setting into place the new leader. As God's holy appointment of leadership was recognized and honored, the congregation witnessing all this could sense and understand the weighty significance of this event.

Pastor Dominic also realized the spiritual significance of what was happening. He recalls, "Pastor Dowdy chose to give me articles of faith: a sword to signify the

There was going to be a shift from my command to his command—with all of heaven's authority behind this transaction.

authority of a leader in command and a prayer shawl to signify the office of a prophet and a man of prayer. This was a passing of an inheritance and heritage of leadership (sword) and faith. These items were strong symbolic tokens illustrating that her mantle was now imparted to the new leader."

Based on my understanding of Scripture and of the dynamics taking place in the heavenlies, I delegated, released, and gave part of my authority to Pastor Dominic Yeo as the new leader—just as God told Moses to call together the leaders and to delegate part of his authority over to Joshua. I blessed him and felt led to speak two things—exponential increase and exponential finances—into his leadership.

That spiritual transaction was recorded in the heavens, and God has honored and fulfilled every word that was released and spoken that night: the latter glory shall be greater than the former!

Chapter 14

Waking Up to a New Day

DURING MY TIME AS TRINITY'S senior pastor, I always had a ministry that extended outside our local church. There was always a Macedonian call to train pastors and leaders in other nations, to help them build strong churches. God said that there was a breakthrough anointing upon me that had to be imparted to others. All this was exciting. Yet the reality was, there always seemed to be more churches and organizations to be helped than I had time for.

With the leadership transition process in full gear, I knew it was the time for me to shift into a new level of ministry, to do the things God had placed upon my heart. I had some ideas and thoughts about what I might be doing. It would involve moving to a whole new level—where I would not just work with leaders, but with *leaders* of leaders.

Remember what I said at the start of this book. The divine assignments God gives us are often really stepping-stones to the greater things He has in store for us.

Leadership transition and succession does not mean that you will not continue doing what you love. More likely than not—if you have discovered your gift, passion, and anointing, you will be using these gifts, but in a different expression or in a larger capacity. I would say it this way: *Same mission, different expression.* For others, it could mean moving into new areas and soaring in new directions that you have never explored.

The challenge before us is to imagine a future beyond where you are now, and what you have already done. For those of us who have reached a pinnacle of success (been there, done that), this can be tough. But don't be fooled; God *always* has something more ahead for you. He is calling you to move on and move up.

New Vision

Ideally, you should lay the groundwork for this next chapter of your life before the handover, so that by the time you transit and exit, you will have formulated a new vision for your next lap.

To break through to the next level, it will be important for you to identify and define the new you. Who are you now, and who are you becoming, as you move on and move up into God's next season for your life? Don't be confined to the safe and the familiar. Break out from the box—that narrow, limiting definition of who you are and what you do.

Allow God to stretch your imagination and your self-definition. Let God begin to expand the possibilities so that you can envision a dramatically different future, and answer the question: what will significance look like at this new stage of my life?

Some marketplace leaders find that significance in their new chapter means leading a nonprofit organization or volunteering in an area of passion. Some find that they can leverage their years of experience to become a consultant. Others find it liberating to engage

The challenge before you is to imagine a future beyond where you are now and what you have already done.

in missions work or interdenominational ministry that they did not have time for previously. Some pastors follow their passion to train emerging leaders in a Bible school setting. Still others will find a second career in speaking, teaching, or training.

Break Out of the Box

The point is this: do not limit God. It is time to throw it open and tear up the boxes and narrow categories you have confined yourself to. Do not stay locked up in the box; break out of it and allow God to do a new work in you. Naturally He will start with where you are—but He will also lift you to new levels of significance. Don't miss this: take time to hear from Him, to be in the Word and let God redefine you.

For me, my vision had not changed, but I was now pursuing and fulfilling it at a new level. In the past, my focus had been on the development of leaders; how to disciple, mentor, and release them. Now God has

Who are you now—and who are you becoming—as you move on and move up into God's next season for your life?

opened up a whole new level of leadership development.

God strongly impressed this upon me: whom do

leaders talk to, and who can they share their struggles and heartaches with, as they face the challenges of leading in these turbulent times? Here is where God began to use the combination of my age (which is a secret) and my many experiences in life and ministry at a new level and in new ways. He has positioned me such that I now spend more time with leaders of leaders.

A Reflection Exercise

Take time to reflect and receive God's dreams for you in this new season. You will need to consider:

- What are your aspirations for this next phase of your life? What would your ideal life look like?
- What are your spiritual gifts? What have you always enjoyed doing?
- What prophetic words have been released over your life? What is God saying, and how is He leading you?
- How would you describe, in your own words, your life's mission and purpose?
- Look back over the years of your life: How has God used you? What have you built?
- What experiences has God taken you through that could now be used in a wider arena, or translated into lessons that would help/encourage others in the same position? This could be a time for the convergence of your diverse gifts and experiences.
- What will be the *expression* of God's gift in you after you no longer have your current title?

- Does the gift God has given you need to be upgraded? Should you consider taking some courses or a series of short seminars to upgrade and sharpen your skills and knowledge for your next phase and the expression of your gifts?

Evolution of a New Identity

Defining your new identity is vital because you cannot tell people how you can serve them until you are sure of who you are and what you can offer them. You need to have your "elevator speech" ready, to have a clear and

Take time to hear from Him, to be in the Word and let God redefine you.

concise answer for anyone who asks you, "What are you doing now?" Here's a rule of thumb: If you can't explain it in a sentence or two, *it's not clear enough.*

This new identity will evolve and get clearer as you go along. Within a year or two, your calling will become even clearer and you may have to rewrite your own résumé. That is okay. You are a work-in-progress, developing and expanding the new expression of your God-given anointing. You are walking in progressive revelation. The key is to take baby steps and make incremental shifts so that you are moving in the direction God leads.

New Structure

Once you have defined your new expression for this season, you will need to determine some practical things. For example:

- **Where is my office?** You will need to decide where you will be working from, whether from an office or at home.
- **What do we call this?** If you are starting a ministry, consultancy, or business, you will need to define the name and identity of this new entity and secure its proper legal registration. You will also need a website, a business card, and method for people to contact you.
- **What is my ministry or business model? What are my income streams?** If you do stay on after the transition to contribute to the organization, there might be a financial package or some support provided for you. If not, then obviously you would need to work out your finances. You may experience some difficulty putting a price tag on your services, especially if you are serving nonprofit organizations, but this is something you will have to work out.

Your new season may require a new structure or framework. For me, in addition to serving Trinity Christian Centre, I birthed Naomi Dowdy Ministries (NDM), and this became a vehicle of my ministry in this new chapter. Through this new legal entity, I reach across denominational lines even further than before.

A few years after my transition, God began to open another door that reached into the area of marketplace ministry. I was in different businesses before I came into full-time ministry, and in this new season, God began to use me again

Naturally God will start with where you are—but He will also lift you to new levels of significance.

in this area. As this developed, I registered a new business called Naomi Dowdy Mentoring and Consulting (NDMC). Through NDMC, there are contracts and measurable time frames for me to serve different companies and organizations.

New Relationships

Developing new relationships is essential at this stage. If you are going to rise to a new level, you will have to get out of the same closed circle in which you have been. It was a good circle but now God is pushing you out of your comfortable nest. Yes, transition is a time when you also celebrate and cherish old friendships, but for you to make that shift, you will have to expose yourself to new people and new thinking.

Get outside of your present cocoon and emerge into a whole new level of interaction and experiences. You should work on networking, mixing with new people, going to new gatherings, and exploring relationships outside of your present parameters.

You may also need to re-establish old acquaintances. Even if these are people you have known for many years, your relationship with them must be developed at a new level and on new terms.

The reality of your relationships in this season is that they are based upon respect, honor, and your value or ability to render ongoing contributions into people's lives and ministries. This goes beyond positional influence, into the realm of leadership influence. When you are functioning at the new level of significance, you lead because of influence and not because of a formal title or perceived power.

Divine Connections

Some of these new relationships will be divine connections that God brings into your life to get you going in your new season.

For many years, people had urged me to write a book, so as to share my experience with a wider audience. At that time, I had not yet authored a book, and in the midst of my busy schedule, I had never gotten down to actually doing it. After I made my transition, I was connected to a book editor who helped me get started on my first book. Now, after five books, the prospect of writing books is a lot less scary!

If you have heard from God, you can be sure that He will send

For you to make that shift, you will have to expose yourself to new people and new thinking.

you the resources that you need for your new season. But first, you need to get out there and develop those new relationships, so that divine connections can be forged.

It's a new day! God has new opportunities waiting for you. Never look back. If you do, you can become as "frozen" and petrified as Lot's wife. You must release the old and embrace the new season. This is the time to define your legacy more definitively than ever before.

Your latter *shall* be greater!

Your Next Level: Significance

ALL OVER THE WORLD, I see the need for the baton of leadership to be passed to a new generation. It is time for the changing of the guard. It is time to release a fresh wave of God's glory and power into our churches. It is time to stir up a fresh vision for new possibilities!

What needs to happen? We need to get out of the way and let God move. This is not merely a transfer from the older to the younger. God is raising a new breed of leaders. God is calling for a new generation of Samuels who will lead in such power and anointing that the spirit and perception of God's people will shift into high gear, and entire nations will be impacted.

What an awesome privilege you have as God's agent for change! You are God's chosen leader to commission and anoint the next generation of warriors who will go forth to take the land. It is time to pass the baton!

Friends, there is more at stake than our immediate success. Past generations built things up and then just gave them over—releasing everything into untutored hands—and walked away into the sunset.

Now God is saying, "Enough is enough. We have wasted money, time, energy, and lives with this model. It is a new day. Now I am calling an experienced generation of leaders who are older, wiser, and more experienced. I am calling them to step out of their comfort zones and to release their churches and organizations over to Me. Train, disciple, and equip a younger generation to take your place so that you will be free to serve as my ambassadors to the nations—to help, encourage, and upgrade other leaders in the current ways of God just like Paul did when he went to the city of Ephesus."

At this juncture, it is vital for you to distinguish between success and significance. Moving into the season of significance does not mean just *you* being significant. Rather, it is about adding to the significance of others. That is the only way we can be truly significant in the kingdom.

> *Moving into the season of significance does not mean just you being significant. Rather, it is about adding to the significance of others.*

Avail yourself and your wise counsel to the younger ones so they do not keep making the same mistakes over and over again. Then voluntarily step aside and release them—and step into God's new season for you.

As you, and countless other global leaders, choose to do this, I see an exponential increase in leadership development and transitions—and soon this movement will reach epic proportions.

Let's stop repeating the same mistakes and losing more time. Let's determine to stand together and declare to Satan: "The blinders are removed and we are going to invade your territory and open the prison doors that are binding our future leaders. We will release them into God's high calling and defend them along their journey."

The time is now. It is high time to break out of the old rhetoric and hear God's call to move on and move up from succession to significance.

Come on, move on and move up to your next level—I will meet you there.

Is God calling you to move up to the next level?
These books will help you get there!

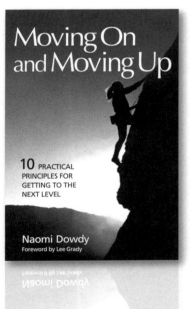

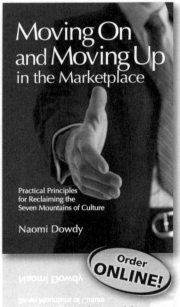

How I wish there were more Naomi Dowdys in the world!
If anyone is qualified to speak on the subject of moving to a higher
level in God, she is a prime candidate. This important book
will equip you in many practical ways to move to the next level
and to become the leader you were called to be.
— J. Lee Grady, editor of Charisma magazine

Also by Naomi Dowdy

Books
Commissioning
Moving On & Moving Up*
Moving On & Moving Up In the Marketplace*
Strength To Stand

* Also available in Chinese and Spanish

Audio Teachings
Aligning Two Worlds
Alignment That Secures Your Future
Alignment – The Key to Authority
Becoming a New Wineskin Church
Declaration for Transformation
Divine Alignment for Divine Assignment
Healing
Kingdom Giving
Kingdom Growth*
Living & Leading in Turbulent Times*
Lost Identity, Discovered Destiny
Paralyzed or Powerful?
Priesthood of the Believer
Refresh Your Anointing*
Return to Pentecost
Revelation Knowledge
Taking Hold of God's Promises
The Cross – Rediscovering Its Power for Today
What Can I Do For You?*

* Also available online as instant downloads

Order online now **www.naomidowdy.com**

Leadership Mentoring with Dr. Naomi Dowdy

For Business Owners, CEOs and Marketplace Leaders

Leadership is a lonely journey. Business leaders often find it difficult to talk to someone in confidence regarding issues in the business, their family, or even their own lives. Christian business leaders find it doubly challenging, especially as they endeavor to integrate faith and business. Executive or life coaches are limited in their capacity to appreciate the issues faced by Christian business leaders, and the advice they give seldom aligns with the Word of God.

But now there is a platform where you can seek counsel from an experienced spiritual advisor and coach — Leadership Mentoring with Dr. Naomi Dowdy.

About Dr. Naomi Dowdy
Dr. Naomi Dowdy is no stranger to entrepreneurship and business. Having founded and led several organizations of global impact, she has an in-depth understanding of the issues Christian business leaders face on a daily basis. Her spiritual counsel, leadership mentoring and apostolic covering have helped business owners and CEOs move up to the next level.

One-to-One Leadership Mentoring
This Leadership Mentoring will provide you with:
- A Leadership Mentor and Personal Coach who is committed to help you succeed in life and business.
- Apostolic covering, practical guidance and prophetic prayer support as you ride through the blips of business, and take the risks necessary to expand your business.
- A Spiritual Advisor who will journey with you and help you step into God's promises and destiny for your life.

- A Visionary Strategist who will provide input and inspiration for pioneering business models that combine profitability and Kingdom purposes.

These one-to-one Leadership Mentoring sessions will help you identify and resolve issues in business, family, and life. Confidentiality is strictly preserved.

Consulting and Speaking Engagements
Dr. Naomi Dowdy is also available for:
- Consultation regarding the restructuring and realignment of organizations and companies.
- Speaking engagements at events organized for business people, teaching on God's purposes so that business people can be established in their calling and embrace their role in Kingdom transformation.

Contact:
Dr. Naomi Dowdy
USA: P.O. Box 703686, Dallas, Texas 75370
Singapore: Tanglin P.O.Box 48, Singapore 912402
Tel: (65) 6304-7766   Fax: (65) 6743-9608
Email: info@naomidowdy.com
Web site: **www.naomidowdy.com**

www.movingonmovingup.org

Be among the new breed of Kingdom men and women who are moving on and moving up in God!

Find inspiration and resources for:

✓ Moving Up to the Next Level

✓ Navigating Transition

✓ Expanding Your Kingdom Vision

✓ Fulfilling Your Divine Assignment

Log on now and get a free e-mail course on Navigating Transition!